HEAVEN AND EARTH

Making the Psychic Connection

JAMES VAN PRAAGH

POCKET BOOKS

New York London Toronto Sydney

POCKET BOOKS
A division of Simon & Schuster, Inc.
1230 Avenue of the Americas, New York, NY 10020

Copyright © 2001 by Spiritual Horizons, Inc.

Originally published in hardcover in 2001 by Simon & Schuster Source

ISBN: 0-7432-2726-3

First Pocket Books printing November 2002

10 9 8 7 6

POCKET and colophon are registered trademarks of Simon & Schuster, Inc.

For information regarding special discounts for bulk purchases, please contact Simon & Schuster Special Sales at 1-800-456-6798 or business@simonandschuster.com

Front cover photo by Jeanne Strongin

Designed by Alyssa Taragano

Printed in the U.S.A.

To Ethel
Who showed me glimpses of heaven
as we walked together on earth

CONTENTS

IN APPRECIATION

To all the people who have demonstrated the trueness of their hearts and the brilliance of their light.

Especially:

LINDA. Your dedication, love, commitment, honor, loyalty, professionalism, and incredible laugh have helped me more than you will ever know. Thank you from the bottom of my soul.

BF. Thank you for filling my life with excitement, wonder, appreciation, and opportunities to experience and learn the various aspects of timeless and unconditional love.

DOROTHEA. You have touched me with your undying devotion in opening the eyes and hearts of many with your sacred works of healing.

MICHAEL. Your words of wisdom and your gentle teachings continue to evolve my heart. May each step you take be filled with fulfillment.

CAROL. This journey would have never happened if you hadn't opened the door. You have been a guide and a true and loving friend, who demonstrates love in all you do.

MRS. RED CLOUD. Thank you for reminding me of the many roles love and forgiveness play in incorporating the wholeness of who we are.

JOE AND JACQUIE. Thank you for watching over me with integrity, honesty, and friendship—I am forever grateful for friends like you.

SABENA. Not only am I forever blessed by your healing hands, but I am also honored by your commitment to and deep compassion for the human condition.

And to *all* my friends who stay behind the scenes, thank you for your trustful and ageless love. I hope I come somewhat close in returning the joys you have brought me.

JAMES

PREFACE

Since the publication of my first book, *Talking to Heaven*, in 1997, I have had the good fortune to travel around the world and share my message of life after death with thousands of people. I am still amazed at the number of people who are eager to learn more about psychic phenomena. Although many know the buzzwords (mental telepathy, clairvoyance, aura, and entity), they don't really understand what these terms mean. Many lack personal experience with such things; others experience them but can't identify what they are. Throughout time, shows featuring mediums and, today, movies like *The Sixth Sense* only intensify our curiosity about the spirit world. People want to make contact with their loved ones and seek validation of their own experiences with the spirits. They want to know that these are *real,* not figments of their imagination.

This book is intended to help you learn as much as possible about the world of spirit and to decide for yourself what is true or false. By drawing from personal experience, I hope to teach you how to hone your basic psychic abilities and sharpen your sixth sense. I also include testimony from others who have been touched by angels and visited by spirit guides.

More important, I have included exercises that you can practice to expand your own psychic awareness. As you progress, remain flexible and open. Some experiences you may have on your journey may be unusual or upsetting, but as you go, you will learn to understand and handle them. Each person develops in his and her own way, and at his or her own pace. Don't get discouraged when things don't happen right away. Remember: It took me years of trial and error and effort to be where I am today. As you learn to develop your psychic talents, using them will become a way of life.

For years I have been teaching that death is not the end of existence, nor is it something to be feared; there is indeed life beyond this physical world. Earth is only one part of a vast multidimensional universe. Spirit beings from other worlds are around us all the time. These spirits serve the human population in many ways, as teachers, companions, creative inspiration, and protection. It takes courage to look beyond our three-dimensional world and know that something greater exists. The more deeply involved you become with the spirit world, the more your habits and conditioning will change, and the more your life will become focused.

Let this book be your guide to developing your natural psychic gifts, to experiencing spirit contact first-hand, and to empowering yourself to live a better life. It is my desire that everyone experience the profound connection between heaven and earth, and that this book help you do so.

chapter 1

THE AWAKENING

*Tapping Into Our Senses
to Achieve Psychic Awareness*

Living in New York in the late 1970s was one of the most exciting and educational experiences of my life. Disco was king. Platform shoes and feathered hairdos were in. I had signed a lease for my first apartment, and felt at long last that I was free and had no one to answer to but myself. It didn't matter that the apartment was located near Needle Park, a neighborhood where all the drug addicts hung out. Or that the patter of feet I heard at night belonged to rats scampering across my kitchen table. Or that the view from my window was of an old elevator air shaft. No matter how little I had, it was all mine.

I was twenty years old and ready to take a bite out of the Big Apple. Looking back, I am convinced that living in this kind of environment assisted me in becoming keenly aware of both external stimuli and my own inner voice. A young kid living in a dangerous part of the city had to be on his toes and rely on his senses.

At this stage of my life, I was not yet involved in psychic phenomena—especially not communication with the spirit world. Aside from my occasional *feelings* about things, I didn't give much thought to the psychic realm. It wasn't something that had affected me personally since childhood. But my outlook on "the sixth sense" would soon change forever.

At the time, I was a student at Hunter College and worked nights as a stagehand on Broadway to supplement my income. Four days a week, I would take the subway to Grand Central Terminal and then transfer to an uptown train to Hunter College at 68th Street. If I timed it correctly, I had just a minute to catch a doughnut at the shop a flight above the platform before my train arrived. I would get on the second to the last car, where there were plenty of seats available. Because it was a pretty short ride, I would spend the time staring off into space, much like the rest of the passengers, and let myself be lulled by the rocking and rolling of the train.

Sometimes I would eye the passengers, doing a quick study to guess where they were going and what their lives were like. Like me, there were one or two regulars who sat in the same seat every day. After several months I got to know one of them. Her name was Millie Johnson. She was a seventy-one-year-old African American woman who stood five feet tall in her stocking feet. She would often say, "I was taller in my younger days." After a while Millie and I looked forward to seeing each other's faces in the morning.

Over the course of several months, we learned a lot about each other. Millie lived alone. Her husband,

Horace, had "gone on to heaven" years earlier. She had a fraternal twin named Margie who lived in Atlanta, but they hadn't spoken since their father had died twenty years earlier. Margie accused Millie of running off with their father's inheritance. I was convinced it was a miscommunication that had been left unresolved all these years, that they could and should reconcile.

Millie took care of an elderly gentleman from her church. She left home at five in the morning to take the train downtown. After she served him breakfast and cleaned up a little, she would take the subway back home.

Millie had a way of telling stories of her beloved Horace. "I know he is still looking after me," she would say. She often also wished aloud that her sister and she would talk, and she regretted not having had children. "I know those are the cards I was dealt, and I do my best to play them," she said.

One Monday something seemed very different. When I entered the subway car, I looked around for Millie but didn't see her anywhere. I sat down and wondered where she was. It wasn't like her to miss a day. I figured she was under the weather. I spent the rest of the ride scanning the billboard advertisements above the seats. I stopped at one in particular: WANTED. It was a picture of two men. As I read the sign, I learned that these two men were wanted for an attack on a train passenger. The moment I looked up at their faces, I heard a voice in my head say, "Take her home." I didn't know what this meant, so I let it go and spaced out for the rest of my ride.

The remainder of the week went by without my friend Millie. I started to feel uneasy. I didn't have her phone number and didn't know where she lived.

The next Sunday night, I was up late, desperately trying to finish a term paper. I went to bed about three in the morning, hoping to complete the project during my midmorning break the next day at school. At 6:00 a.m. I jumped out of bed with an urgency to get to school early. I knew the library would be open, and thought I could get some work done. I don't know how to describe the feeling I had, but suffice it to say it was a clear sense that I had to get to school right away.

At seven-thirty I entered the uptown train and was surprised to see Millie sitting there. She was equally startled to see me. "What happened to you?" I asked. She told me that she had received a letter from her sister, and explained, "She came to New York to see me." Millie and Margie spent the week mending hurts and catching up. I thought it was very odd that we happened to meet at that particular time and cracked some joke about the cosmos.

The train pulled up to Millie's stop, and as she waved good-bye to me, I felt a push to get out of my seat, and heard those same words, "Take her home." Wondering what they meant, I got out of the train and escorted Millie up the stairs. She made a fuss about my missing the train. Because it was the dead of winter, it was still somewhat dark outside, so I thought it was a good idea to walk with her. There was not a soul on the street. Then I *knew* why I was there. As we turned the corner, I saw two sinister characters huddled in the doorway of a building. When they looked at me, the thought of being mugged crossed my mind. They seemed familiar, but I didn't know why. I just shook my head and quickly ushered Millie away. Halfway down the block I realized where I had seen those faces before. They were the two men staring down from the WANTED poster on the train.

If I hadn't paid attention to that intuitive voice, and hadn't been keenly aware of my surroundings, I might not be around to tell this story and neither would Millie.

Like me and my *feeling* on the train, many of us have hunches about things and later realize that our hunch was right. Maybe the phone rings and you know who is calling before you pick up the receiver. You might have had a déjà vu experience—something that you felt you experienced exactly the same way before. Most of us have had these kinds of experiences—they are some of the simplest examples of psychic phenomena. Imagine how much better your life would be if you could rely on this inner sense to make the right choices and succeed in your goals.

I believe that everyone has psychic awareness, but few have the patience, understanding, or, perhaps, the desire to develop it. Even though I was psychically aware at a young age and could see things others could not, I did not develop my psychic abilities to their fullest until I became an adult. With the help of like-minded people and books on the subject, I began to teach myself how to tap into the world of spirit at will. A lot of patience, and years of practice and development, went into the work I do today.

Unfortunately, most of us go through life without using this wonderful, innate, God-given ability. It's no wonder our lives can seem so difficult, or even dull. We don't listen to the thoughts that fill our minds, and are oblivious to the consequences of our actions. We face life with apprehension, and don't understand why certain things happen. Instead of finding peace and pleasure, we find stress and struggle. Inevitably, opportunities are missed, problems mount, and relationships split apart. We settle into a routine, and like it or not, we get used to it. Our birthright—who we are and what we are made of—lies dormant. We are walking through life without sensing it fully.

The truth is, everything you want to know is already inside you. You just haven't remembered it. Instead of feeling lost, abandoned, or confused, I want you to recognize that you are a spiritual being who is part of a large cosmic family of spiritual beings. As you awaken your innate psychic ability, you will begin to connect to your spirit family. The spirit world can be extremely insightful to your day-to-day life. There are many spirits standing by, willing to help you remember who and what you really are.

In this day and age, it has become all too easy to bypass our own spiritual inheritance and turn to others for answers, especially psychics. And while many psychics are conscientious and high-minded, there are others who are egotistical and prey upon human frailties. One does not have to have high moral character to be psychic.

This leads me to a very significant issue concerning psychic phenomena. One of the most important discussions I have with my students is about conscience and commitment. As you cultivate and expand various psychic skills, you must also develop a sense of responsibility. You have a responsibility to yourself and to those with whom you have a psychic connection. By responsibility, I mean that you use your sixth sense to enhance your life and the lives of others. Using your psychic power to control or hurt others or to cause fear or predict disaster is irresponsible and will most likely have karmic repercussions. So will using your spiritual connections to acquire wealth or prestige or to impress others, or for any other egotistical gratification. Remember that everyone generates energy. If your motivation for improving your psychic ability is for some personal gain or negative end, this energy will go out from you and come back to you. You cannot protect yourself from your own negative energy. It is your own creation.

There are three things you must do when you begin your journey of psychic development. First, you must set a goal for yourself. Second, you must be dedicated to reaching your goal. This means taking the time required to practice, meditate, and understand the subtleties of a new language. Third, you must trust your ability. Remember that spirit is always available and ready to help you. Use it well.

THE FIVE SENSES

Let's get started. When interpreting the signals from the spirit world, you must perfect your sensitivity to such an extent that you can see with your inner eye and hear with your inner ear. The world is full of distractions; it takes patience, practice, and determination to sit quietly and listen to your inner voice. To do this, you must broaden your use of the sensory skills you already have.

Most of us learn to apply our five senses the minute we are born. When we are babies, we don't have the words for the things we see; someone tells us, "This is a ball." Or, "That is a train." The same is true for our sense of hearing. We learn to interpret the sounds we hear because we hear them over and over. Your mother says your name as she looks into your eyes, and you soon understand that when she says "Jimmy" or "Alice," she means you. You learn the sound a dog makes when it barks, and what a door sounds like when it slams, and you begin to integrate this information into your sensory vocabulary.

For each sensory organ there is a corresponding spiritual or astral sense organ. We are spiritual beings first and foremost, and when we incarnate on earth, we go through a process in which the soul creates a force field of mental and astral material around itself. Therefore, we are made of a synchronistic union of psychic (mental and emotional), physical, and spiritual energies. Our senses often work to bind these energies.

Sight

We use our eyes more than our other senses. When we think of someone, we usually see an image of that person in our mind. Our memory is filled with images and visual symbols from the past. Since our sight center is the most active, it is only natural that our corresponding psychic vision center would also be the most active. We only have to exert our minds a little more than usual to awaken our psychic vision.

I am a clairvoyant, which means that I see visions or pictures in my mind's eye. My mind's eye is my third eye center, the chakra located in the area of our forehead between our eyes. When I see spirits, I see them with this third eye vision, as if I were looking at a movie screen inside my head. Most psychics use this type of inner sight when they work. However, it is also possible to see an image or a vision outside the mind's eye, as in "seeing a ghost." There have been occasions when I have seen such apparitions take form, but it is rare. Mostly I see through my third eye center as if I were seeing an impressionistic painting or a moving picture.

Dreaming is one way to develop our psychic visioning. When we dream, scenes, images, colors, and objects are trying to relay messages to our minds. Often these messages have to do with everyday issues that we are trying to resolve; sometimes they may be trying to warn us of a future event. We often meet our spirit guides and deceased loved ones in our dreams. Becoming cognizant of our dreams by writing them down and learning to interpret the dream images is especially helpful in opening the third eye center. Dream visions can also provide us with clues and answers to some of life's mysteries, such as "What's heaven like?" and "What happens when we die?"

Mental telepathy is another way to use psychic vision. Telepathy is the psychic ability to see a person, object, or scene that is at a distance and out of view, like seeing something taking place in another city. Telepathists can see into the past and future because they see events that are remote and beyond normal recollection. Telepathy can be used in many contexts, to gather information from sources most people don't have access to. Edgar Cayce was a telepathic healer. While in a trance, he used his psychic vision to diagnose diseases that he had never studied and to describe treatments in which he had no formal education. He had a remarkable gift, and his legacy is a constant reminder of the inborn power that we all possess.

Sound

Hearing, like vision, is another sense we use constantly. Clairaudience, or clear hearing, is much like clairvoyance, only we hear sounds with our psychic ear that are not within physical sensory reach. As with clairvoyance, clairaudience relies on the exertion of our minds to hear beyond the usual. Concentration is a key factor in cultivating psychic awareness. When you hear clairaudiently, your astral ear is attuned to the higher vibrations of spirit, and can hear beyond the normal range of sound, much like a dog can hear a high-pitched whistle inaudible to human ears. "Hearing voices" and "clairaudience" are not necessarily one and the same. Certain mental disorders cause people to hear voices. If you hear a voice inside your head and it tells you to do something destructive, I would suggest that you see a psychotherapist. Clairaudience, like clairvoyance, must be tested over and over again. Clairaudients can hear voices, names, and even music. Some of our greatest composers were and are clairaudient.

Smell

Our sense of smell is reportedly the first of the five senses to be developed inside the womb. Scientific research points out that our sense of smell is located in the limbic region of the brain, where emotions and memories are stored. It is no wonder that certain odors or fragrances can transport us back in time to some childhood event or happy occasion like our first love affair. I remember one summer day: I was out in my garden and a certain aroma evoked a memory from early childhood. Suddenly I was once again playing in the yard with my brother—clear as day.

We have all had similar experiences. For instance, it is not uncommon to remember the perfume our mothers wore when we were young—when we smell that fragrance at a department-store counter, memories of her come flooding back. Or to remember the smell of something else we associate with her. Every time I smell vanilla, I think of my mother baking cookies. The perfume industry takes advantage of the fact that fragrances evoke emotion and memory. It spends a great deal of time and money trying to perfect a scent that will become a financial blockbuster, and uses scent-oriented emotional cues in its strategy. In the last few years, aromatherapy—with its magical smells in candles, lotions, and oils—has earned enormous popularity. That certain smells can lead to emotional well-being has been demonstrated by the number of people who use aromatherapy scents to relax, to get energized, and even to excel in their studies. Our sense of smell is indeed a powerful tool.

Certain fragrances assist specifically in psychic perception and spirit contact. Lilac, lavender, chamomile, frankincense, rose, and lemon have long been used by individuals to alter consciousness and attract higher vibrations into their environment. The study and use of floral and herbal scents will enrich your psychic development.

Pay attention to the odors around you. When a deceased loved one wants to communicate with you, it is quite common to smell something associated with him or her. Perhaps it is the aroma of a woman's perfume or the odor of a particular brand of cigarettes. Often these scents are dismissed by our logical minds as some lingering, stale aromas around the house. In actuality, spirits do try to comfort their loved ones through scent. I often respond by saying, "If you smell a loved one's perfume, she is definitely close by."

Touch

Touch is another sense that can be developed as a psychic tool. Think about it: When a stranger shakes your hand, do you get an immediate sense of what he or she is like? If not, this may be a good thing to start paying attention to. A person's grip can provide insight to his or her personality.

Psychic healers use their sense of touch to locate disease in a person's body. This is known as the laying-on of hands. They can pick up hot or cold spots that signify imbalance. When we touch a person's body, we exchange energy with him or her. Massaging certain points in the body helps to alleviate pain and discomfort and to release cellular memories from our tissues. Many modern physical therapies that utilize touch—like Rolfing, shiatsu, and reflexology—help people eliminate physical toxins as well as psychological and emotional traumas.

Psychometry is another way that our sense of touch is utilized. Psychics employed in police work often use psychometry to get information about a case. They are able to hold an object and get certain impressions from it. Each person, place, and thing is filled with the God Force energy; someone who is sensitive enough can perceive a connection between the energies of an object and the person using it.

Taste

We are less familiar with the powers of touch, smell, and taste than those of sight and sound because we rely on them less often; they are no less intense. Often when I am doing a reading, I feel a spirit's presence even through my taste buds. For example, if a spirit is trying to communicate a suicide by gunshot, I will have the taste of metal in my mouth. The same is true of reading situations involving alcohol or cigarettes, even medication. A spirit will bring forth this type of sensation as evidential validation of its existence. We never know through which sensations a spirit will send a message. Developing all our senses can only help us discriminate between what is ours and what is spirit's.

How do we develop our senses so that we can attune to the higher levels of experience? We can start by paying attention to everyday details. As we become aware of our surroundings, our thoughts, and our actions, we are instructing our minds to know more.

Ever notice that some people are always in the wrong place at the wrong time, while others are in the right place at the right time? Or that someone you know is always coming down with a cold or ailment while someone else never gets sick? Or that someone has many healthy relationships and others have few or none at all? The universe is not random. The God Force energy that sustains us and permeates every atom of existence does not pick a chosen few to enjoy a charmed life and leave the rest of us to struggle to get by. We all have the right to be in tune with the universe and to partake in the goodness that life has to offer. Everyone has the potential to expand his consciousness beyond physical awareness into psychic dimensions.

If you want to tune into the spiritual world, you must wake up to the life around and within you. You have come to earth with a spiritual life plan, and you are here to fulfill your destiny. With the help of angelic beings, spirit guides, and your deceased loved ones, you can avail yourself of all the creative inspiration you need as you journey through life. Your endeavors into the psychic realms will not go unrewarded. I promise.

THE UNQUIET DEAD

I never know how spirit will use me, or through which sense I will interpret its signals. When initially picking up psychic information, I get a sense of *knowing* about something. Once I attune myself to the energy in my environment or to the person for whom I am reading, the first things that come to mind are scenes being played out as if in a movie. A scene may consist of a place, or several people in various forms of dress, or an individual showing me something about himself or a particular situation. During practically all of these experiences, I am bombarded by sight, sound, and feeling. Then I link together the pieces of information transmitted by the scenario in order to understand what the spirit is trying to communicate. The following anecdote shows one way I utilized my senses to shed light on what turned out to have been a particularly gruesome situation.

I had moved to California, and I was still in the early stages of my work as a medium when I received a phone call from an anxious woman. She spoke in erratic breaths as if she had just finished a marathon. Her name was Katherine.

"A friend of mine gave me your number. She had a reading with you last year," she said. Katherine continued to talk to me in short, staccato sentences. "I've never called a psychic before. I don't know if you can help me or not. I hope you can. My friend thinks you can. This is all so strange to me." Without a moment's pause, Katherine went on, "I'm at my wit's end. You're my only hope."

Finally I had a chance to speak. I described my background and psychic abilities. She didn't seem to want to take the time to listen.

"I can see you in two weeks," I offered.

"Oh, no, you have to see me sooner. It's a matter of life or death."

That was the first time anyone ever expressed such urgency to me.

"Please, Mr. Van Praagh, I am desperate. I have nowhere else to turn." It sounded as if she were about to cry.

I looked at my schedule again.

"I can see you Saturday morning at about eleven," I told her. "Come to my house—" I was about to give her my address when she interrupted.

"No . . . no, you must come here to my house. You have to see for yourself," she said.

I agreed to go to her, and wrote down her address. I suggested some simple meditation exercises to calm her mind before I arrived, knowing it would be difficult for either of us to get the necessary results if she didn't.

Saturday morning came. As I drove down the beautifully landscaped, tree-lined streets of Beverly Hills, I couldn't help but notice all the attractive and expensive houses, and wondered who lived behind the walls of such opulent estates.

I meandered down Katherine's street, looking for her house number. I remember how pleasant I felt surrounded by such pristine beauty. As I approached her block, any sense of serenity I possessed vanished. My enjoyment of elegance and charm was overtaken by an overwhelming sense of doom. The strange and hostile energy I felt was much more overpowering than the loveliness of the area.

I stopped the car, got out, and looked around. On the opposite side of the street stood Katherine's house. It reminded me of newsreels of bombed-out cities. The grounds were muddy and desolate. In place of an orderly lawn and a kaleidoscope of blooming flowers was a front yard littered with construction debris. I looked again at the paper in my hand to confirm that I had reached the right address, even though in my heart of hearts, I knew this was the place. I was right.

I felt a sense of foreboding. I looked up at the rooftop. Something was wrong. The gables were all crooked. The two chimneys also tilted, reminding me of the Leaning Tower of Pisa. I thought, Something strange is going on here.

Katherine's crackled voice interrupted my observation. She was standing in the driveway "Thank God you came. I didn't know if you would come or not. Isn't it awful?" she said, looking toward the gables. They loomed over us like an ugly face.

"Yes. I don't understand. What's the problem?" I asked.

"They won't let me build it. No matter what I do to it, they undo all the work," she said in her staccato rhythm.

"Who's *they?*"

"That's what I want you to tell me." Katherine escorted me through the chunks of concrete that lined her driveway toward the back of the house. At first look, the house reminded me of a Cape Cod–style bungalow from the early 1930s, but it seemed to have had many incarnations since. We stood in the garage, which appeared normal enough even with remnants of ongoing construction piled along one side.

Katherine began to explain her predicament. "My husband and I bought this house three years ago. Since that time, we got divorced. My husband was eager to rid himself of this house, so he gave it to me as part of the settlement. Before our divorce we hired an architect and made plans to renovate. The contractor began the project, and after a month the work seemed to have one delay after another. Nothing was getting finished."

"Well, that happens a lot," I commented.

"But you don't understand. The work was done, but then it was undone," she said in an exasperated tone.

"What do you mean?" I asked.

"After something was finished, it would be undone. Like after we installed the windows, the very next day half of them were cracked and had to be replaced. A week after laying the tile floor, the ground underneath buckled, and all the tiles came apart. We haven't been able to put a floor in yet."

"Okay, I'm beginning to understand," I said, still perplexed.

Katherine continued. "I have been through three contractors and a team of subcontractors. No one is able to finish any work. I'm at my wit's end." At that moment her face went dead pale. "Then there was the roof. It was almost done, and I actually started to feel somewhat relieved. It was the last day of work, and one of the roofers lost his footing and actually fell *through* the roof. Here was a man with thirty years' experience in the business!" she exclaimed. "We had to call the paramedics. Thank God, he's all right."

I didn't say a word.

Katherine spoke again, trying to shake me into action. "Mr. Van Praagh, this is not normal. Someone is trying to prevent me from finishing this house."

My mind was racing to find logical explanations for so many obstacles. Then suddenly, as if something were literally pulling me, I was compelled to turn and face the house. At that moment, I knew that this was not going to be one of my usual spirit connections.

I took a deep breath and closed my eyes. I began surrounding myself in white light and quietly uttered a prayer. I requested special help and protection from my spirit guides. The more I was able to raise my energy vibration, the more I felt the pull of the negative force around Katherine and her house. The menacing energy was growing stronger. I knew it was time to begin.

I turned to Katherine. "Let's go inside."

We entered the house through the back door and stood in a pantry facing the kitchen. Almost at once, I felt a piercing chill run up my spine. Some invisible something met us in the kitchen. Katherine's face turned another shade of pale. Right then and there we both *knew* we were not alone. Katherine looked at me for some sort of explanation. My eyes were as wide as hers, but I made an attempt to shed some light on the situation.

"Many times, when a discarnate soul is nearby, you can actually sense a coldness in the room. This is due to the change in vibration, or the slowing down of the spirit body. Don't worry," I said to calm her. (Meanwhile, I thought, What did I get myself into?) "Just give me a moment to gather some more information."

As if in slow motion, we walked down a hallway leading to the front of the house. A lingering feeling of unease numbed my bones. With each step, the unseeable energy became more heavy and unsettling. I felt as if something were crowding in on me, sort of the way one feels on a subway platform during rush hour. There seemed to be no place to move, so I stopped where the force felt the strongest. I could tell that it was distinctly male energy and that it was threatening. At that moment, I saw with my mind's eye the embodiment of the dread we had been feeling. In the center of the hallway stood four rough-looking men. Their blank eyes stared grimly ahead as if they were looking right through me. Two of them had beards. One was gray-haired; one was bald. Their hate-congested faces were as clear as day. Meanwhile, the intense negative vibration grew stronger. These men were intimidating, cruel, and ruthless. As I continued my gaze, I received a thought that a man was murdered right where I was standing. In my vision, I saw one of the four holding a gun, and smelled the vapor of smoke, as if someone had just lit a match.

I felt Katherine shaking me back into the awareness of the room as she said, "Mr. Van Praagh, are you all right?"

I jolted from my trancelike state, feeling cold and clammy. Perspiration dripped down my face.

"Can I get you some water? You look like you've seen a ghost!" Katherine exclaimed.

I turned to her and said, "Someone was shot here. Right here in this hallway."

I looked at the wall behind me, and there it was—a small bullet hole etched on the surface.

Katherine covered her mouth in horror.

I continued to tune into my senses so I could find out more details. "This person was brought to a basement. Is there a basement in this house?" I asked.

I could tell that my statement gave Katherine a start. She stared at me and slowly spoke. "Yes, there is."

For the record, basements are rare in Southern California.

Katherine led the way, and we walked to a door, which led to another door underneath some stairs. This second door led down to a basement, just big enough for a few people to walk into.

"I feel a man was shot and then dragged to this basement and buried," I said.

Katherine nervously looked around the small concrete room.

I went back to the main hall, blinking my eyes to bring myself back to my center. When I looked down the hallway, the four men I saw a moment ago were gone.

As I walked toward the front door, I had a feeling that told me to look up. On the stairway there was another spirit. This one was wearing a white coat like a doctor. I knew I had to follow him.

"Stay behind me," I cautioned Katherine.

With each step up the stairs, the coldness that I had felt earlier returned. This time it was ice-cold and even more foreboding.

There was a high-pitched buzzing in my ears.

"What is that?" shrieked Katherine.

"I hear it too!" I replied.

The noise was coming from a room at the end of the upstairs hall. It sounded like kittens screeching to be fed. I followed the white-coated doctor toward the room. He walked through the wall and disappeared. Cautiously I moved closer to the doorway. By now Katherine was holding on to my shirtsleeve.

When I reached for the doorknob, she pulled my arm back. "This is the room that has given us the most trouble. This is where the roof collapsed. I also found feces in this room."

I knew this was the vortex of the strange and destructive energy. I sensed something emotionally unstable. I felt a mixture of anger, hatred, and pain coming from the room.

Normally, when I see good energy, it appears gold or white to me. When energy is filled with negative emotions, it looks dark gray, red, or black. This is what I was seeing as I walked through the doorway.

The temperature was now so cold that we could actually see our own breath. Katherine's eyes were filled with fear. Her body was shaking, and she looked to me for security.

I did my best to reassure her. "It's okay. Just try to keep your emotions in check. The more frightened you get, the more the fear will fuel the negative emotions present in the room."

"I don't want to go any further," she said.

"Okay. You stay outside, but I need to see what this is all about." I walked into the center of a completely empty room. I looked around and surveyed the space. The drywall, exposed pipes, and brick were illuminated solely by the hole in the roof. I centered myself by taking a few deep breaths, and then began to attune to the vibration of the room to see what I could pick up psychically.

After my third exhalation, I started to smell something foul. It was the stench of burning hair, and it made me sick to my stomach. The sound of muffled voices broke the silence, and gradually these voices grew into screams and shouts. I shook my head from the disturbance. Then once again the doctor in the white coat came into view, along with the source of the mournful laments. When I saw the entire picture, I stood frozen as if nailed to the floor.

In the center of the room was a man strapped to a table. The man looked up at me with bulging eyes—his

gaze beckoning me to help. He mouthed the name
Victor. I assumed he was trying to tell me his name. The
doctor stood over Victor. It looked like a scene from
Frankenstein. The man in white was prodding his subject
with some sort of electrical current in very precise and
calculated movements. I realized that I was witnessing
incredibly cruel and inhuman torture, too horrible to
imagine. I had to rub my eyes to force myself back to
the present, then quickly exited the room.

It seemed like only minutes passed by, but in actuality, two hours had elapsed since my arrival. I rejoined
Katherine outside the house and explained as clearly as
possible what I had experienced.

"It seems as though a doctor once lived here and
was somehow involved with illegal or criminal activity.
He tortured people either to make them divulge information or to force them to keep something secret."

This insight, as cold-hearted as it seemed to me, was
surprisingly acceptable to Katherine. "Mr. Van Praagh,
that makes a lot of sense."

"Why do you say that?"

"Because when I first moved here, one of our neighbors told me about the history of the house. She mentioned that the person who owned it fifteen or twenty
years ago was a doctor of dubious character."

My mouth dropped open in amazement.

"He supposedly kept to himself, but she said there
were always different cars parked in front of the house.
She even saw the police a few times. Apparently, there
were calls from the neighbors about disturbing noises
coming from inside the house."

I had heard and seen enough for the day. All I wanted to do was go home and get some rest. "I'll be back tomorrow to do a house clearing. We have to get rid of that energy, or you'll never finish your house."

As promised, I arrived the next morning. When I entered the house, the energy already seemed to be lighter. Walking into each room, I cleansed and transmuted the negative vibrations with the pureness and love of the God Force energy.

As I began my work on the top floor, I listened to eerie sounds coming muffled through the door, and slowly I turned the knob. Several entities were crouched in the corner. They were shaking with fear and trepidation. "We're trapped here," they cried.

I psychically sent them thoughts that they were free to take their own space. When spirits are bound to earth like this, they will invade the space of living beings because they feel they have no space of their own. It was important that I help them to realize that they did indeed have their own energy. I visualized a ball of light around them, filling their energy space for their highest good.

Then I spoke out loud but gently. "Your feelings of entrapment are not real. You have passed out of the physical into the spirit world. You are free to go into the light."

Within minutes the room was brighter, and the cold air dissipated. The warmth and light of sunshine replaced the shade of fear and terror. The house was *clean*, and Katherine would at last be able to finish her renovation. (In Chapter Nine, I will describe what to do to clear a house of unwanted energy.)

Because I am a mental medium, I use my mental faculties in combination with my senses to perceive spirit. In the case of this haunted house, I was able to see a spirit standing in a room. In my mind's eye, a spirit appears as if it were solid, yet I know that it is not a physical being. The vision of the spirit is being seen by my *spirit vision* in my third eye center. The same is true for my hearing voices and smelling odors. All of these sensations are filtered through my mind and seem real to me.

The use of our senses plays a key role in unveiling the work of spirit in our lives. By the simple act of paying attention to everyday details in your life, you can begin to open the gateway to your psychic ability. The more you become aware of your surroundings, the more you train your mind in seeing, hearing, feeling, touching, and tasting, the more you pay attention to your thoughts and actions, the more you will build awareness. When we are unaware, we sleepwalk through life, living a dull and inactive existence, no matter how busy we think we are. When we are aware, we are truly alive and have a better understanding of life on its many levels.

Clear understanding and communication can only be attained when you release the negative mental and emotional baggage stored in your physical and psychic space. I will go into this idea in depth in the next few chapters. In time, you will be amazed at how your own psychic energy can travel across space and time to heal and help those in need. You have the privilege of being a channel for the God Force energy. Let your sensitivity guide the way.

chapter 2

THE SIXTH SENSE

*Using Intuition to
Receive Information From Spirit*

First of all, let me say that we are born with six senses, not five. The sixth sense, the one most of us don't know how to apply in everyday life, is our intuition, inner voice, or psychic awareness. We all have this power, but for many people it remains repressed. Our sixth sense relies on our intellect, our five senses, and our emotions, and works in conjunction with any or all of them. Not only do clairvoyance, telepathy, and other psychic phenomena filter through our intuition, but artistic inspiration, mystical religious experiences, and creative problem solving do too. All are aspects of intuitive functioning.

Intuition is a sense of *knowing*, and this knowing comes from within. This sense of knowing is spontaneous; it is not a question of analysis. If you put too much effort into trying to be intuitive, you will impede the process. In other words, intuition is not something that you can make happen. It just happens. You *can* learn to become aware of it happening. Intuition occurs when our minds are relaxed and not concentrated on a particular job.

Usually when we let go of a problem, the answer we seek comes through. For example, I have a habit of misplacing my keys. It's a common occurrence. And as soon as I stop looking for the keys, there they are. It's the same with intuition.

Everyone has had an intuitive experience. For example, maybe you were thinking of a certain sweater you wanted to buy for someone. You happen to walk down a street you usually bypass, and there in a store window you see the exact sweater, *and* it's on sale! Something led you to go down that street to that store to find that particular sweater. That something was your intuition. It can lead you to finding the right thing at the right time, and it can lead you to the spirit world.

Often people think of me as some sort of miracle worker, but there is nothing superhuman about speaking with the dead. The only difference between me and you is that I have learned to use my sixth sense incredibly well. Like other people who are considered psychically gifted, I have merely learned to distinguish my inner voice and the voice of spirit from the multitude of opinions and beliefs swirling through my mind. Any psychic will tell you that it takes observation, reflection, and trial and error to develop a strong intuitive sense.

Think of the first time you tried to drive. You had to begin with the basics, study and listen to the instructor.

The first time you sat behind the wheel, you had to distinguish the accelerator from the brake pedal and become familiar with what happens when you put your foot on either one. You learned how to slow down, to stop, or to go in reverse. Intuition is like any other skill. The more you use it, the better you are at it, the more confident you become, and the smoother the journey. You will find that using your intuition will enhance every aspect of your life.

Yes, perhaps some have a special inclination toward psychic awareness and some have refined it to a master level, but just the same, everyone has intuition. Like everything else in life, it is up to you to train your intuition to whatever degree you are willing to reach for.

I am frequently asked, "How do you know that it is spirit giving you information and not your own imagination?" In the beginning of my development as a medium, this was the hardest thing to determine. Like everyone else, I was so used to listening to my mind for the answers that at first it was difficult to *rethink* information that came through—which is necessary in order to discern between my own mind chatter and the information coming from spirit. To be discerning, you have to pay attention to yourself. I usually tell my students, "To thine own self be true." In order to get in touch with this sense of knowingness, you must begin by having an intimate relationship with yourself. The more you understand your own motives, ideas, and beliefs, the easier it becomes to separate what is yours from what is spirit's.

INTERPRETING INTUITION

There are many levels of intuition, just as there are many levels to ourselves. No one pattern fits every person. Start with interpreting your thoughts and feelings. You will have to be honest with yourself. You, more than anyone else, must know what's going on inside you.

On the physical level, we may feel bodily sensations warning us of danger or threat. For instance, a friend of mine named Penny told me about a time when she was planning a trip to meet her daughter in Paris. From there, they were going to rent a car and tour the South of France. She had made her plane reservations and car rental arrangements and bought several tour books to take with her. About two weeks before her departure, she began having terrible stomach cramps. They came out of the blue and didn't connect to any illness.

She said, "I had had that problem once before. I think it's fear, like a warning system in my body." The cramps persisted, but she decided to go on the trip anyway. "I wasn't afraid of the plane crashing, but I knew it had to do with the trip."

When she arrived in Paris, it was raining.

"It rained most of the time we were in France, and I wondered if that had anything to do with the cramps. But I didn't think so. Finally, the answer came the last week of the trip. We were driving into Cannes, and it was still raining. I had stopped for a red light at the bottom of a hill. When I looked into my rearview mirror I saw this car barreling down toward us, and I knew it wasn't going to stop in time. I turned my eyes forward and said a quick prayer just as the car slammed into our rear end. Luckily, I always made sure that my daughter was wearing her seat belt. If she hadn't been this time, she would have been hurled through the front window. As soon as the car hit, I knew that this was the fear I had been feeling. In a way, I was relieved because it was over. My daughter had to be taken to the hospital, but she was all right, just had a neck strain."

"Wow," I said when she finished.

"James, at that very moment when I looked through the rearview mirror, I knew that this was the reason for the cramps. I also knew that it had to happen, and there wasn't anything I could do to prevent it. The accident was a karmic lesson, and I understood what it meant."

Bodily responses are definitely a source of intuitive information. Learn to listen to them, or at least notice them. As for my friend, she was a very aware lady, in touch with herself and her feelings.

I know there are times when I want to say something to a friend, and when I go to say it, the words just don't come out. At that moment, I know that my intuition is telling me to keep my mouth shut. Perhaps it isn't the right time to say what I want to say. Becoming aware of the sensations in your body is just another step toward self-awareness and total intuitive awakening.

Just as the physical body sends us messages, so do our emotions. People often tell me that when they first met their husband or wife, they knew he or she was the "the one." Usually this happens in spite of preconceived notions about one's ideal lover. My friend Andrew said that when he met his wife, "she wasn't the kind of woman I usually dated. I like blondes; she was brunette. I like petite women, and she was tall. But something told me she was for me. It was her humor that attracted me. I later realized it helped me overlook some of the traits that don't normally appeal to me. But after just one date, something else told me to see her again. I knew that first night she was the person I was going to marry."

We have all heard the term "woman's intuition." It doesn't mean that only women have intuition. It means that women are more in touch with their feelings than men, or haven't suppressed them as men are taught to do. Emotions change from moment to moment. There is a difference between emotional ups and downs and intuitive feelings. However, in order to differentiate the two, we must get in touch with our feelings and learn the difference.

On the mental level, intuition usually comes in images. This is the level of creative problem solving. Inventors often claim that their inventions come to them in daydreams, night dreams, or when they are not focusing on the problem. People in top management positions usually say that they get a "gut feeling" about a certain decision. The ability to know intuitively what will succeed definitely adds to a person's success rate in business. We've all had that "Aha!" experience when something buried deep inside us comes to the surface. We're sitting at the hairdresser's reading a magazine article, and suddenly the answer to some task at work becomes crystal-clear—again, an example of how intuition can rise spontaneously without effort or strain on our part.

Last but not least, there is such a thing as the spiritual level of intuition—the mystical experience of knowing. This is the glimpse into the true reality of our existence. Moments of spiritual intuition are unforgettable.

A friend of mine once told me of her experience at a silent retreat. At the time, she was involved in a spiritual organization that had property in Lake Arrowhead, California. "We would go for a week, sometimes two weeks. There were no indoor sleeping arrangements, so we had to bring sleeping bags or tents and find a spot on the hillside to bed down for the night."

The people in her group took turns cooking meals, prayed together in a sanctuary, and spent the rest of the time in silence. "James, after days of being silent in nature, I had an incredible experience. I saw myself getting on a train with thousands of other people, and I realized that it was a love train—as silly as it sounds. I knew at that moment that we are all made of love and that love is the ingredient or energy that permeates the whole world. I felt so at peace. There was nothing I had to do to be better than I already was. I *knew* that I was love."

That is true spiritual insight.

Mystical experiences like my friend's have no purpose other than to transform an individual's view of reality. The practice of meditation is essential to attaining this kind of spiritual intuition and to communicating with the spirit world.

Like our other five senses, intuition must be integrated with our intellect in order for us to translate the information it is sending. Physicians who have spent years in medical school do not bypass their medical knowledge and rely solely on intuition. However, combining both sources of information can uncover medical problems that are difficult to diagnose by conventional means.

When you begin to listen to yourself, perhaps for the first time, you will discover there are layers to your awareness. After filtering the superficial encounters, you will reach the deeper levels of your being. Confusion clears away, and trust takes its place. The beauty of intuition is that no outside force compels you to do anything. You just know. From that intuitive point, you can make clearer choices.

Once you are aware and relaxed, and the mind chatter has fallen into the background, the next step is gaining receptivity to your feelings. When you deliberately set out to identify feelings, you will be amazed by how quickly they will come to your immediate awareness. Repressed feelings make it very difficult to tap into intuition because they cause enormous tension in the body. Furthermore, these emotions are usually attached to something that has already occurred or is yet to come. When you live in the past, or are worrying about the future, you are not living in the moment, and intuition occurs in the present.

Intuition is received and interpreted differently by each person. People often ask me, "What was it like when you first became aware of spirit?" And, "Was it a physical sensation?" I can honestly say that when I am impressed with spirit, my whole being senses it. I feel some sensation in my body, but certain specific senses are impressed. In my case, I see and feel the presence of spirit beings because I am a mental medium who uses clairvoyance and clairsentience. However, like most mediums, I can recognize a spirit's nuances in every part of myself. Again, this has to do with awareness. One must become aware of the differences between desires, fears, and true intuitive feelings.

Once, I was driving in Italy and found myself all turned around on a road to nowhere. I tried to figure out the road signs but wasn't doing a very good job of it. As I waited at a red light, a truck drove by with the word REGINA painted in bold letters on its side. I turned and followed the truck, and it led me right to the town for which I was searching. I knew it was a sign from spirit because my mother's name was Regina. She was sending me help in a way that I would understand.

CHILDREN'S NATURAL INTUITION

At a young age you might have associated psychic feelings with day-to-day expressions and behaviors, like happiness or sadness. But those psychic feelings were real to you even if there was no adult to tell what they were or were not. The meaning of these feelings could only be labeled after the same situations repeated themselves and the same feelings were experienced. However, as you got older, you were taught to depend less on this *feeling* sense and rely more on your rational self or objective mind.

This *feeling* is part of the subjective mind, the unconscious or subconscious layer of self that has neither logic nor visibility. An old saying teaches us, "Seeing is believing." We are told to rely on what is tangible. Closing your eyes, getting away from the objective mind, and quieting the senses is one way of reacquainting yourself with the inner voice of truth.

When I was a small child, it was quite natural for me to experience intuitive impressions. Like most sensitive children, I assumed that everyone could see or feel things in the same way. For me, it was quite normal. Only when I was told that what I perceived was not typical did I realize that I was different. I had a very vivid imagination. I would create scenarios in my head and act them out in my room just like most children. However, there was always a fine line between imagining things and picking up on things on an intuitive or psychic level. Because I was a child, I was not aware of how to control these impressions, nor how to interpret them. It was often confusing, and sometimes scary.

THE MASKED BANDIT

When I was eight, my best friend and neighbor Frankie and I spent every Saturday morning doing the same routine. We would wake up early, eat a bowl of Sugar Pops while watching cartoons, and then scream across the fence to one another to come out and play.

Robbie, another friend of ours, and Frankie's sister Jeanne also joined us, and the four of us would venture forth into the day anticipating wild new adventures. We did the usual kid things like climbing trees, pretending they were spaceships, and taking the roles of spacemen or robots invading the earth. We had fun traveling the cosmos, which was neatly contained in some eight hundred square feet of my backyard.

One night, Frankie and I decided to set up a tent in the backyard just the way we had seen it on an episode of Mutual of Omaha's *Wild Kingdom*. Snuggled in our sleeping bags, we began to tell each other ghost stories. Naturally, we were always trying to outdo each other to see which one could be scared the most. It was my turn, and I prefaced my ghostly yarn with the words, "This is a true story."

"In this neighborhood there is a man who goes around during the day and sneaks a peak into people's windows. He checks the windows around the house to see if any are open. If there are, he usually comes back late at night to rob the people's house."

"What are you talking about? Nobody does that," Frankie said.

"He sure does. Wanna bet?" I retorted. "This guy wears a red handkerchief around his nose and mouth. All you can see are his eyes, beady and black as a bird's."

Frankie started to fidget. He was not very fond of birds after seeing a horror movie about them.

I whispered, "If he catches you looking at him, he will take you away, and you will never be heard from again."

That seemed to be enough storytelling for Frankie. He zipped his bag over his head and murmured, "Let's go to sleep."

The next day we were startled out of our dreamland by the sound of Frankie's mother screaming from inside the house. "Frankie and Jamie, get in here right now! Come on, it's time to come inside!" she shouted.

We untangled from our sleeping bags and slowly made our way into the house. We wondered what all the commotion was about. As we walked inside the door, Frankie's mom ran over and knelt down in front of us and embraced us in a tight hug. "Are you boys okay?"

"Yeah, Mom. What's the matter?" asked Frankie.

Then we heard the sound of a police siren and the muffled sounds of people's voices coming closer.

"Last night a burglar climbed into Mrs. Clarke's house through a bedroom window and hid under her daughter's bed. When her daughter rolled over, she saw this man grab her purse and jump out the window."

Both of us stood there stone silent.

Frankie looked at me, and I shrugged my shoulders in complete surprise. "Did she see what the guy looked like?" he asked.

"Mrs. Clarke said he was wearing a red handkerchief around his nose and mouth."

Our timing couldn't have been more perfect. We gasped in unison.

"She said that her daughter was so scared because he stopped to turn and look at her. All she could see were his eyes."

By now our mouths were hanging open in total disbelief.

As I hurried out the back door, I uttered, "I think I better go home now."

That day when I returned home, I told my mother about the story I had made up the night before.

She looked at me and smiled. "It's just a coincidence, Jamie."

I never really understood all the information I received on an intuitive level. As a child I was just open. And I didn't judge or rationalize it like most adults.

A PICTURE FROM SPIRIT

Another intuitive experience happened when I was in the second grade. We had just finished lunch and were at recess. To me, this meant an hour to color. I always had a box of crayons and a pad and would find a place where no one could bother me. I don't know why, but I was always drawn to certain colors like blues and purples. Crayons were magical sticks and the keys to another world. My mind would drift off as I began to color. After a while I would finish my drawing. When I looked down at it, I usually knew it was some kind of scene, but I wouldn't even be sure what it was.

On that day in second grade, I brought my drawing home and showed it to my mother. It was a picture of an upside-down bicycle with a little girl sitting next to it. "Why did you color one leg red and the other blue?" she asked.

I shrugged. I didn't have a reason.

In the picture, there was a streetlamp next to the bike. In the background I had drawn a women looking at the girl. In front of the woman were lots of flowers.

My mother looked at the picture and told me, "It's very pretty."

She put it on the kitchen counter, where she kept all my latest works of art.

One week later, while I was sitting on the living-room floor watching TV, my mother called me into the kitchen.

I got up and ran to her. She had the drawing in her hand. I knew by the look on her face that something had disturbed her. "How did you know?" she asked, shaking the paper.

"Know what, Mom?" I said.

She held the picture for me to see. "The picture you drew. This is your sister."

"What do you mean?"

"Yesterday your sister was riding her bike around the corner and hit a streetlamp. She scraped her knee badly, and a lady brought her home, just like in the picture."

I didn't really think anything of it. "I just colored what I saw in my head," I said, and turned back to the TV.

This kind of thing occurred to me many times as a child. I never deliberately attempted to receive infor-mation, and I did not try to rationalize where it came from. Even now, when I receive psychic information, I try not to interpret it, because I don't want to color it with my own bias.

THE DEVELOPMENT CIRCLE

By the time I became an adult, I had dismissed the many psychic incidents of my youth and, like most people, set goals for the real world. That was until I had a reading with medium Brian Hurst. He told me that one day I would do what he did. Soon after, I began to read many books on the occult, but I was still not sure what to do with my own psychic awareness. I decided to seek Brian's help.

"What do I do next?" I asked. "I don't want this to take over my life."

Brian suggested that I participate in his development circle in order to learn the mechanics of mediumship. "You will have to learn how to keep the door to the spirit world open and also how to close it when you don't want to receive its messages."

Through the development circle, I learned not only how to establish a relationship with the spiritual dimensions, but also the various ways in which the spirit world sends messages to earth. Most of all, I learned the importance of the work I do. I vividly recall the words that Brian said on my first visit to the development circle. They have stayed with me ever since.

"James," he said, "the most important element of

being a medium is the motivation behind what you're doing. Do you want to be of service to the human race? Can you bring an understanding and awareness that we are more than just our physical bodies and that our consciousness survives death? Do you want to open people's hearts to love, understanding, and forgiveness? If you can answer yes, then and only then are you ready to sit in a development circle and merge with the spiritual realms."

People have often mistaken sitting in a development circle as simply sitting around a table in the dark and holding hands. That is the farthest thing from the truth—a Hollywood misconception of spiritualism. There's a lot more involved.

Our development circle took place once a week and began with a prayer. The prayer helped everyone to focus the energy of the room into a unified place of sacredness. It was like singing a hymn before a church service. When you sit in a development circle, you aspire to the highest characteristics of your nature. The prayer was our statement to the universe that we were in unison in our endeavor to bond with spirit.

After the opening prayer, we learned how to meditate. Meditation is the key to developing the sixth sense. The idea behind development meditation is to first quiet the noise of the mind and fully relax the body. In that way, you can begin to release the stimulus from the outside world and feel an awareness of the inside world. This is where your Higher Self resides. The connection to the inner world and Higher Self is through your breath. Breath is the energy of life. The first thing I had to develop was a relationship with the rhythm of my breath.

As I learned to delve into the rhythm of my breathing, I was able to hold the focus of my breath a little longer each time. Slowly but surely, the day's problems and desires washed away, and I was drawn totally into the breath. Closing off the daily grind, I began to experience a rush of thoughts. Each time, I acknowledged the thought, let it go, and brought myself back to my breathing.

As the weeks and months progressed, I became very aware of energy soaring up and down my spine. I was also able to sense this energy encircling everyone else in the room. This is when I discovered that I was sensing the aura.

After several months I began to sense random thoughts and whispers racing through my head. I also began to experience a heightened sense about myself, and at the same time, about every person sitting in the circle. Next, I started to see in my mind's eye the shapes of spirit beings standing around the group. When I focused my awareness on these forms, I would see flashes of faces. Later I would describe what I saw to the other participants in the circle. Sometimes someone else had envisioned the same thing. Each week I became more aware as I continued to practice this mental and emotional psychic detection. When not seeing spirits, we would sit and attune ourselves to the energy of the person sitting besides us or any other type of energy in the room.

Week after week, we sat faithfully in our circle, and

little by little we progressed in our psychic awareness. At the same time, the spirit world had an opportunity to participate from the other side. Because we were consistent, spirits showed up and used our weekly ritual to practice transmitting messages to us. I discovered that spirits have to train their abilities just as we have to master ours. A spirit is usually drawn to someone for whom it has an affinity. Remember that, "like attracts like," and spirits, like people, will gravitate to someone they understand and who they feel will understand them.

As I stated earlier, when sitting in a development circle, you must participate with the highest of ideals and not get caught up in the glitz of psychic phenomena. The purpose is to bring about the highest spiritual qualities for all concerned.

The development circle is really the only place to practice and learn to expand consciousness and blend your energy with that of the spirit world. The more I took the time to practice this communion with patience and cooperation, the more I was able to guarantee a better-quality mediumship. Gradually my connections grew stronger and stronger.

THE MULBERRY TREE

A year after joining Brian's group, I started my own development circle. I gathered together a harmonious blend of people whom I already knew. Lesley, Annette, and Peter were the perfect choices. It was as if we were destined to be together. This group of like-minded individuals were willing to assist me in uncovering my intuitive abilities as well as discovering their own.

Our development circle met every Tuesday at 7:00 P.M. To assure the success of our circle, we adhered to certain rules. First and most important, we met consistently every Tuesday night at the same time. It was our standing appointment with spirit. Second, the same people came every week. We did not interchange one person with another. The spirit world insisted on such protocol so that it could continually build the energy of the circle. Not only would new people diffuse the established energy, but the spirit guides and chemists would have to go back to square one and reestablish the energy in the room every time. Third, it was important that we sit in a circle, alternating male and female, in order to balance the energy.

During the week, and especially the day of our circle, we kept our minds in positive and enthusiastic states. It is much easier for the spirit world to get through when you are in a positive, loving vibration than when you are in one of negativity and pessimism.

After greetings and salutations, we sat in our circle, always sitting in the same seat as the week before. I began each evening with an opening prayer:

> Mother, Father, God. We want to ask your blessing on our circle tonight and ask for a blending of the highest truths of spirit to embrace us and use us according to your divine will. We ask for your assistance in developing

our innate knowingness and to trust in the language of the heart. We thank you and bless you.

After the opening prayer, we would each contribute our own prayer and thank spirit for the opportunity to work with it. Everyone had to actively participate in the connection to the spirit world. We were not there to sit passively and watch someone else do the work. For the next forty-five minutes to an hour we sat in silence. During this time we would meditate, allowing various impressions and thoughts to flow through us.

These impressions occurred in phases. Usually the first phase consisted of changes in the temperature and energy around our bodies as spirit guides began to adjust themselves to our auras. While our guides were doing this, they were constantly transmitting thoughts, feelings, and visions to each person in the group. Most of the time, this information was aimed at someone specific. I found that at first the information did not enter smoothly, but as the weeks progressed, the messages became more distinct. The second phase began when I directly felt my thoughts being taken over by a spirit. I made sure I paid attention to everything that I was experiencing on these other levels so I could recount them at the conclusion of the circle. Third, I sensed when the energy from the spirits started to pull away and the spirit beings had left our space. These energy shifts happened gradually over a period of several meetings, but we were all successful in becoming aware of the nuances of spirit contact.

After the spirit energies had dissipated, and everyone

returned to conscious awareness, we recapped what we had experienced, no matter how trivial it might have seemed. Usually we would record our sessions so that if something was said that later proved to be true, we would have the opportunity to listen to how the information came through.

On one particular occasion, Peter shared his impressions with the group. "Actually, it was really odd. In my mind's eye, I began to see a mist in the corner of the room that swirled into sort of a ball. This ball began to grow larger and larger and moved to the center of our circle. The next thing I knew, it looked like a man kneeling on one knee. His arm was propped up on his knee and his hand under his chin. I thought it very strange, but kept looking to see if I could recognize anything about him. His features became more apparent until I was actually able to see him, clear as a bell. I recognized his appearance from pictures I've seen in history books. It was Sir Thomas More. I thought, Why are you here? I had no particular connection with him. Next thing I knew he disappeared."

Everyone in the room thought this was incredible. Without skipping a beat, Lesley spoke up. "Wait a minute. I know what that means. At least I think I do. I grew up in a part of London near the Thames River where there are lots of squares. In the middle of each of these squares there are beautiful gardens. When I was a little girl I used to go to a particular garden near my house and sit under this giant mulberry tree. This tree was supposedly hundreds of years old. I don't know why I was drawn to it, but I felt safe there, and I would sit under it for hours and sometimes I'd even fall asleep."

"And?" I asked, not understanding the connection.

Lesley continued. "Well, legend has it that Henry the Eighth and Thomas More used to rest under that very same tree."

The moment she said that, everyone took a breath.

"What do you think he wanted?" I said, breaking the silence.

Peter responded, "The feeling he gave me was a sense of warmth and affection and approval. Was he an important symbol in your childhood?" he asked Lesley.

"Well, maybe. When I sat under that tree, I used to dream of coming to America to be able to live and work here. It was something I always wanted to do," Lesley declared. "America meant freedom to do whatever one believed in. Maybe that's the connection."

"I think Sir Thomas More came here tonight to confirm that you made the right choice," answered Peter.

A DOCTOR BY MY SIDE

There were many evenings when deceased family members came through, and we would give each other messages or impressions of such a spirit's thoughts. The most memorable moments, however, were the times our spirit guides presented themselves. One evening, a guide of mine by the name of Harry Aldrich came to me, or rather *through* me. I had fallen into a deep trance.

When I awakened, Peter said that he, too, had seen my guide in his mind's eye and described him for all of us. "He was wearing a brown English tweed jacket and had a cloth cap and gold-rimmed glasses."

"We got it on tape," said Annette. "Listen for yourself."

I had gone into trance only a few times before. This time, I didn't even think we had been sitting very long. However, we were in the room for close to an hour. Annette played the tape, and we all sat back and listened to the voice speaking in a distinctly English accent.

The voice said: "I am the man who is helping to keep this medium's mental and spiritual bodies in rhythm. I was known as Harold Aldrich and practiced internal medicine in London. I wished when I was on your earth that I could have aided those in need, but alas, time can certainly be man's fiercest foe. I will tell you now that this man has work to do, for he is a teacher to many souls. He is here to show others how to love. He is a very strong spirit, and many will want to drain him mentally and physically. I ask you all to be vigilant of his well-being, for his message is an important one. As a group you create a love force that is strong enough to permeate the ethers."

The tape continued as Dr. Harry informed us that he would assist me in helping others heal emotional and physical imbalances. He would also help keep my energy clear. Dr. Harry made it clear that Peter should act as a mentor to me in getting the word out about life after death through a book I was destined to write. He mentioned more than once that he was the representative of a team of spirits from the other side of the veil.

When the tape was over, I was dumbfounded. I looked around at everyone and said, "Well, I guess that means I have some work to do, eh?" I said a closing prayer and thus ended our extremely eventful evening together.

Intuition plays an important role in channeling higher energies. We have all had a feeling about something but then dismissed it as a dumb idea. Later we realized that our hunch was right, and that we missed an opportunity because we trusted our logic more than our intuition. I've seen this happen a lot in relationships. Patience and persistence are the keys to discerning between our own thoughts and those of spirit.

There is no doubt in my mind that you are already using your intuitive power. Perhaps you aren't using it as much as you would like. That's okay. The place to start is where you are right now. Developing your own innate psychic awareness comes only with practice and purpose. It is a process of attunement. In essence you are fine-tuning an instrument. In this case, the instrument is your own sixth sense.

chapter 3

THE AURA

*The Energy Field of Light and Color
That Surrounds Us*

Awareness and intuition are the first avenues to the world of spirit. The next is your aura. In my work, I have long been aware of the importance of maintaining a healthy, radiant and functional aura. Being able to view and identify the energy, light, and colors that make up a person's electromagnetic field has helped me understand how our bodies, minds, and emotions are influenced by the condition of our aura and vice versa. This invisible energy field is composed of layers of life-force energy and is ever alive, active, and conscious.

Think of the aura as a brilliant glass shell surrounding your body. From the moment of your conception to the end of your physical incarnation, your aura accumulates every thought, word, feeling, and deed of your life. Like rain, dirt, and dust coating a glass surface, your aura is covered with debris from years of life experiences.

Now imagine that you never clean this glass shell. It would be impossible to see through it. Your visibility of the road of life would be extremely limited. You would be unable to think clearly, you would feel unsure and unsafe, and probably wind up making wrong decisions or none at all. In the end, you would not get where you wanted to go.

The only way to see, feel, do, and live with complete freedom is to maintain your auric shield. Achieving your desires is dependent on the condition of this electromagnetic energy field. As you study the aura and its many layers, your psychic sight will develop gradually and naturally.

THE AURA'S LAYERS

At the time of conception, when the sperm enters the ovum, the electromagnetic fields of the father and mother merge. The ovum will only accept the sperm that absolutely matches her own electromagnetic sphere. That is why I tell my students that no one is here by accident. We do choose our parents. This choice is made by a soul before incarnating to earth. At the very point when both spheres merge, a burst of color is released, creating a new magnetic field that becomes the aura of the human embryo. Cell division begins, and chromosomes form. The word *chromus* is Latin for "color." These chromosomes are your true auric colors.

Within your aura is all the information needed for life, including your genetic and ancestral lineage, a record of your past lives, and the karmic contracts and lessons that you intend to resolve in this lifetime.

Your aura is composed of many layers, or "bodies," (which I have described in greater detail in my book *Reaching to Heaven*). Within these various layers of the aura are energy patterns that affect your physical, emotional, mental, and spiritual selves. As you become aware of the following energy patterns of your aura, you will understand how they can influence you. Learning to recognize these energy patterns will help to expand your psychic awareness.

The Etheric Layer

The etheric layer, or etheric double, is the energy body that closely surrounds the physical body. It is an exact replica of your physical self. The etheric layer acts as a switchboard between a person's soul and his or her physical body.

This is the layer that influences your DNA. For psychic purposes, I believe that DNA contains a pattern of awareness that is forever changing, shedding, and moving forward as best fits the survival of the human race.

From the etheric layer emanates the seven chakras or main energy systems of the human body. Each chakra of the etheric body has its own color, and the color varies in accordance with a person's thoughts, moods, and environment.

The chakras also contain vibratory frequencies, sound, and aromas. They resemble oval-shaped spinning wheels. Each chakra interrelates with the others and connects to every point in our physical bodies. The higher light of the upper chakras nourishes the lower chakras.

Most of us communicate through several chakras at the same time, mainly in the three lower centers—root, spleen, and solar plexus. When we want to communicate from the upper or spiritual levels, we do so through the third eye and crown chakras. For this to happen, the chakras must be operating at optimum frequencies.

In a healthy chakra system, all chakra centers are spinning in a clockwise direction and are all interconnecting with each other. When a chakra system is totally open and functional, it is possible to live on one's own breath without food or water. The energy flowing through such a body is fundamentally clear of all toxins.

Unfortunately, most of us do not have a healthy chakra system. One or more chakras may be completely shut off or spinning in a counterclockwise direction. This is usually due to lifestyle, beliefs, fears, and experiences. When energy is blocked in any of our chakra centers, the physical symptoms of illness appear.

The Astral Layer

The next layer of the aura is the astral body. This layer corresponds strongly to one's emotional state. The emotional layer is concerned mainly with the past. It has a tendency to form attachments to people, places, and objects and is triggered by programs developed in childhood and past experiences.

For instance, a friend of mine lost one of his parents when he was six years old. Losing a parent at a young age can condition a person to feelings of abandonment. This was true for my friend. He kept getting himself into relationships and even jobs where he was either left behind or asked to leave. This only produced more feelings of abandonment for him. It became a vicious cycle until he recognized that he had to deal with the grief of losing a parent. Once he was able to purge himself of his feelings of abandonment as well as the sadness, fear, and anger that went with them, he was able to stop the karmic wheel driven by this highly charged emotional issue.

As you can see, this astral layer operates in alignment with the karmic lessons a soul chooses to learn in each lifetime. We attract specific people into our lives for the purpose of completing karmic relationships.

The Mental Layer

The third main layer of the aura focuses strongly on the future. This is the mental body, and it lives in "what if" land. It strongly dislikes change, and it prefers life to behave in a repetitive manner. Most habits are rooted in the mental body. The mental body can be considered a control freak because it wants to be in charge all the time. It consistently attempts to overrule the emotional body. It cares little about feelings, and pushes one to repeat a certain pattern over and over again.

The mental layer is the home of thought. I have often stated in my previous books and in my workshops that

thoughts are real things. They are as tangible and perceptible as your car. Yet you cannot see them with your
physical eyes. Thoughts are like X rays, microwaves,
radio waves, and electricity. They exist on a different
frequency level from our bodies. Just because you don't
physically see microwaves doesn't stop you from using
your microwave to heat leftovers. Something is at work,
and you are benefiting from it. Thoughts, too, are always
at work, and you can either flourish or flounder because
of them. Thoughts filter through your mental body
much the way radio waves send signals to your TV set.
The mental layer is your connection to the psychic
arena—your thoughts do indeed matter.

Like radio waves, thoughts are vibrational and invisible; they permeate the atmosphere, traveling like electrical currents from person to person. We are like walking sponges, soaking up every thought that our friends,
lovers, children, co-workers, and even strangers have
directed toward us. This can be either a very positive
thing or detrimental to our well-being.

I recognized this phenomenon when I first began
scanning the energy fields of individuals for whom I
was reading. I almost always sensed other people's
thoughts within a person's auric field. A psychic friend
of mine once made a remark that precisely captures
this idea of us as walking sponges. She would often say,
"It isn't *what's* wrong with you, it's *who's* wrong with
you."

Most mediums use the mental layer of the aura to
receive information from the spirit world. The information received from the mental body often appears

imaginary and fantastic, so most people tend to ignore it. However, the more one sensitizes oneself to the nuances and energy of spirit, the more this layer is strengthened, and the more it begins to fulfill its purpose as an interface with spirit.

The Ketheric Layer

The highest body, or ketheric layer, of the aura appears as a beautiful golden light that exists approximately three feet above the surface of the physical body. Within this layer dwells a person's capacity to learn, grow, and heal. All completed soul tasks are registered in this layer—it is the soul's link to the Akashic Records. The Akashic Records are the cosmic details of every person's existence from the beginning of time. Each moment of your life, be it physical or nonphysical, is indelibly recorded into this cosmic consciousness. In other words, the Akashic Records contain every thought, feeling, experience, nuance, dash, dot, and hiccup of an individual's entire existence.

Now that you have some idea of the composition of the aura, you can begin to understand why it is a vital link to our psychic encounters. The aura is our bridge to the unseen. Through it, we are able to attune to the subtler dimensions of spirit. The stronger your aura, the easier it is to receive helpful messages from your spirit friends. The weaker the aura, the more likely you'll draw negative energies and entities into your life.

Each time I do a reading, I attune myself to the aura

of the person across from me in order to access the
spirits around him. I must also make sure that his
energy is properly grounded. This will make the psychic connection with the spirit realms clearer. If he is
emotionally or mentally unstable, it is difficult to get a
clear and open channel to the other side.

The following is an example of what can happen
when your aura is left vulnerable to negative influences
created by your own and other people's thoughts.

THE VELCRO SUIT

A few years ago, a woman by the name of Rachel
came to my office. The moment she appeared, I knew
something was very wrong with her. Her face was pale
and ashen. Her eyes were dull and lifeless. I knew that
she was bringing with her something more than just
herself, and immediately I asked her to sit down so that
I could help her.

"How have you been feeling?"

Rachel replied, "I am a bit more tired than usual. I
have some aches and pains, and I feel restless."

I told her that before I could attempt to contact
spirit, I would like to tune into her energy field to see
what I could find.

"Go right ahead," she said.

As soon as I intuitively focused on her aura, I
became aware of various thought forms that appeared
to be vastly dissimilar to the rest of her vibration.
I determined that the energy around her was not

hers at all, and that it was having a formidable effect on her.

The next thing I saw clairvoyantly was static electricity all around her head. It appeared like fireworks going off in every direction. "First of all, I must say that you are extremely busy. You have a lot of mental energy around you."

Then I saw a variety of colors and shapes around her head and shoulders. "Do you have headaches that originate in the back of your neck at the very top of the spine?"

"Yes," said Rachel. "I usually get them at the end of the day."

"That matches what I am seeing." I continued to survey her auric field and suddenly felt uneasy. I could see dark spiraling balls of energy attached to various parts of her body. At the top of her head I saw a piercing red streak with what appeared to be a screaming face in it. Several small children were clinging for dear life to her heart center. Towards the left part of her head, I saw burning dollar bills. Streams of red and black moved between her throat and her head. This usually indicates a lot of anger present in the individual. Her shoulders looked as if they were being pulled down by a heavy weight.

Then something frightening came into view. I saw a man with a dark brown beard sitting in her energy space. His fingers looked like spikes digging into the top of her back.

"I must tell you that I believe you are a psychic sponge. You tend to pick up everyone else's energy and hold on to it." I proceeded to explain what I was seeing. "Is there someone close to you, a man with a brown beard and green eyes, who is a very controlling individual?"

"Yes," she said, shocked that I could know.

"The image of this man is in your aura, and he is sapping your energy. He is controlling the area around your back," I explained.

"Yes. I know who it is. I have been having backaches ever since I left him."

After I described my impressions in more detail, she confirmed that what I had been telling her was true. "Almost a year ago I divorced my husband, and ever since my life has been a living hell. He has been threatening me and scaring my children. Last week I finally got a restraining order against him."

Rachel began to cry as she articulated the horrible situation in which she found herself. "We had a business together. I found out that he embezzled all our money to give to another woman." She broke down in sobs. "We have three children," she continued. "He told the court I was an unfit mother and that he wanted sole custody of the children. He even tried to turn the children against me. I am so angry, I just want to scream."

"I am so very sorry to hear about your situation," I said softly. "Perhaps if you learn how to take your power back and not let him into your space, you would not feel so helpless."

She looked at me with her big brown eyes. "Can I do that?"

"You know how tightly Velcro adheres to itself?" I asked.

Rachel nodded.

"Well, it's as if you are wearing a Velcro suit. Thought forms and emotional energy like anger and fear come into your space and stick to you like Velcro. That's because your own anger and fears are attracting these things to you. But there is also an advantage to Velcro. You can pull it off when you want to. It's easy. You just have to know how."

I proceeded to describe how to take control of her own energy space by strengthening her aura. Then I showed her how to protect her aura from other people's thoughts and emotions.

"It's important that you practice every day until you begin to gain your power back. Take one step at a time and go day by day until you feel that you have recovered your self-esteem."

After we ended this discussion, I continued with a reading. But in some way, I felt that spirit had already passed on the information she needed to hear.

A WEAKENED AURA

Perceiving auras is different for each person. Some can see the energy vortexes that penetrate the aura, while others see thought forms. Others may only see a part of the aura or a few of its many layers. I personally have seen the various layers, colors, and densities of the auric field. Seeing colors is especially rewarding when you are

healthy and happy. The colors can be totally mes-
merizing—like watching fireworks on the Fourth of July.

On the other hand, when I see an aura like Rachel's
that is muddy, dense, speckled with dark spots, and
filled with a lot of static, I know that individual is holding on to thoughts of anger, rage, violence, judgment,
or resentment. Negative mental energy will appear dis-
colored, muddied, smeared, foggy, and streaked. Ill
health may appear as dirty brown or gray, or dark red.
The extent and intensity of the discoloration indicates
the degree of an individual's sickness.

Emotional trauma, physical pain and sickness, patterns of addiction and substance abuse, negative belief
systems, stress, the loss of a loved one, other people's
energy, lower astral entities, abusive relationships—
these things all contribute to a weakened aura.

Even food can influence the state of the aura. Eating
the meat of animals that have been abused and med-
icated will bring that painful energy into your own system. I'm not saying everyone should be a vegetarian, but
we must understand that the vibration of a living thing
becomes a part of our system when we ingest it as food.
If we would take the time to tune into our bodies, we
could easily assess what foods are right for us.

Too much caffeine and alcohol can wreak havoc on
our auric field. These stimulants can agitate the nervous
system and cause our imaginations to work overtime,
sometimes perceiving things that aren't there. Fruit,
juice, and vegetables, on the other hand, help to cleanse
our system and keep it light.

Negative patterns in your own aura make you vulnerable to the negative influences of other people. It can become an ongoing, vicious cycle. Therefore, it is very important to realize that you are the creator of your own world. Other people's energy will affect you only if you neglect to cleanse, purify, and protect your aura.

DEFECTS IN THE AURA

There are many energetic defects that contribute to a weakened aura, including leaks, tears, impurities, excessive energy, depletion, and decompression.

Leaks

Leaks occur in areas where the fabric of the auric layer has been damaged or has worn thin, and appear like drops of dark ink in clear water. They are generally found in the etheric and astral layers of the aura, but can extend into higher layers when not treated. Leaks occur when there is an injury to the body, surgery, a chronic illness, as well as emotional and psychological shock. They usually cause physical discomfort and, if not repaired, can lead to more severe symptoms, including chronic headaches, back pain, fatigue, abnormal cell growth, and endocrine dysfunction.

Tears

Tears or rips appear to the psychic eye as cracks or holes in the auric fabric. Tears are somewhat more severe than leaks. Most tears are caused by an acute shock or trauma, such as the sudden death of a loved one, accidents, sexual and physical abuse, drug and alcohol abuse, and circumstances that cause over-whelming levels of stress on the body, emotion, and psyche. Tears are serious—they leave you without auric protection. When you have tears in the aura, you may experience chronic fatigue, depression, digestive disorders, migraines, painful and arthritic joints, and immune-deficiency disorders. Aura depletion is a by-product of tears and leaks in the electromagnetic field. This makes you vulnerable to psychic attack, entity control, and sometimes death.

Energy Impurities

Other forms of aura depletion are known as energy impurities which are zones of stagnation and blockage. These areas inhibit the free flow of energy in the aura. Impurities appear in various shapes and sizes and are again caused by negative thought patterns, low self-esteem, anger and grudges, resentment and pain, sub-stance abuse, self-destructive tendencies, and hurtful relationships. Symptoms of energy impurities in the aura may include confusion, obsessive-compulsive dis-orders, manic-depressive behavior, and eating disorders.

Excessive Auric Energy

Constant levels of stress and worry cause excessive auric energy. This appears like static electricity or electrical sparks erupting in the aura, mainly around the head. This is due to too much, or overly dominant, mental energy. As a medium, I am well aware of excessive auric energy. Often, after a lengthy tour in which I am constantly tapping into other people's auras, I contract an accumulation of their released energy. The first thing I usually do when I get home is to clear my aura. If I don't balance myself and release this excessive energy, I very often get headaches and colds. Excessive auric energy can lead to insomnia, back pain, depression, upper respiratory problems like colds and flu, high and low blood pressure, hormonal dysfunction (especially in women), lymphatic blockage, and sinus and allergy conditions.

Decompression

Last, a decompressed aura is caused by all of the above. When your aura is decompressed, you are totally exposed to entity invasion, and any person can plug into your system and siphon off your energy. The emotions that cause the most damage to your energy field are acute fear and desire, both of which lodge themselves in your imagination. If you fear something or desire something to too great an extent, you can become prey to beings in the astral worlds. The best way to help yourself is to stop going over the fixation in your imagination and move your attention elsewhere. Symptoms of a decompressed aura include anxiety, nervousness, thyroid dysfunction, sleeplessness, nightmares, unidentified fears and phobias, shortness of breath, asthma, cardiovascular irregularities, claustrophobia, stomach and digestive disorders, and long-term depression.

UNDER THE INFLUENCE

Many years ago, a young woman named Jane came to my office accompanied by her father. Immediately I noticed huge, gaping holes in her aura. I understood right away why she seemed so downhearted and depressed. She had severe problems that left her weak and unprotected.

I said without hesitation, "You must leave the friends you hang around with."

Jane was taken aback by my blunt comment. I could see that she was extremely vulnerable to other people's opinions. "But how can I? They are my friends."

Jane was acting like a defenseless victim. I had to speak to her like a parent disciplining a child. "These people are bad for you. Their energy is dark and hateful, and they will pull you down to their low level. You have become too dependent on them."

Her father agreed with me. He, too, was quite concerned for her welfare.

"If you do not leave these bad influences, you will suffer some terrible consequences," I insisted.

I suggested some exercises Jane could do to change the energy surrounding her aura. I tried my best to urge her to take immediate steps to leave her so-called friends.

Unfortunately, Jane did not, and perhaps could not,

change her behavior. Two years after our meeting, I learned that Jane was killed in a car accident. The driver was one of her troubled friends, a person Jane felt she could not live without. The friend died too, drunk at the wheel.

What I could see in this young woman's aura told me a lot about her life. Gaping holes, like the ones in Jane's auric field, usually paint a picture of imminent danger. Her friends were what I call psychic vampires. Their negative influence was complicated by Jane's alcohol abuse. The combination of the two weakened her aura to such an extent that lower and unevolved astral entities made a home there. Jane lacked a well-fortified aura to ward off the threat of her friends' persuasive control over her. She needed to take steps to rebuild her power and confidence, the first of which was to release fear. The next was to change her thinking process from one of despair to that of hope and optimism. All of this would have strengthened her aura. At least, she would have had a chance to fight off the negative conditions that dominated her life.

A RADIANT AURA

Even though it is almost impossible to go through life avoiding other people's energies and thoughts, you can strengthen your energy field so that nothing gets through to your space. To sustain an aura that is balanced and healthy, one must nurture thoughts of love, kindness, and especially forgiveness. When your aura is healthy and vibrant, you will likewise exhibit good health, pleasant relations, feel emotionally poised, and have the ability to protect yourself from harm. Have you ever wondered why a pregnant woman seems to have a glow about her? Spiritually speaking, it is the baby's pure, brilliant aura shining through her.

An aura can be so strong that disasters like war, earthquakes, and contagious diseases cannot penetrate it. How did some people survive the Black Plague hundreds of years ago while thousands succumbed to it? Some may attribute their staying alive to a strong immune system. In actuality, it was more likely a strong auric field.

The same could be said for people surviving days buried under buildings after an earthquake. A person's feelings of courage, faith, hope and confidence help to build a strong aura. And a strong aura helps to protect you.

The best way to strengthen your aura is to accept yourself first and foremost as a spiritual being. Daily, practice prayer, meditation, loving thought patterns, kindness, gratitude and respect for self, the universe, and all living beings. This will not only expand this field of electromagnetic energy around *you,* but extends farther and helps to uplift others.

BLOSSOM

One morning before my appointments started, I went into my sitting room to perform my usual rituals to prepare for spirit. As I began to meditate, a beautiful and delightful light blue energy came into my mind's eye. The only way to describe it is to say that I felt as if I were sitting in a garden right after a spring rain. Everything felt fresh and alive. Although I wasn't aware of any spirit in the room, I felt that this energy must belong to someone who would be visiting me that day.

At eleven, the doorbell rang, and a woman named Lynda entered my home. I was immediately struck by her uplifting energy. She had a warm and pleasant smile, and immediately reached out to give me a hug. Usually people are cautious and reticent when they come to see me for the first time. Mostly they are afraid or unsure of what to expect. But Lynda came in greeting me like a best friend. At that moment I knew that it was Lynda's energy I had felt earlier. Her thoughts had reached me before her physical arrival.

The session began with my tuning into her energy field, as I usually do with clients.

"You have incredible energy," I told her. "I feel blessed to be in your presence."

Slightly embarrassed, Lynda thanked me.

"It is such a pleasure to meet someone like you. It is very rare to have someone come here who doesn't carry a lot of baggage with them," I continued.

"That is very nice of you to say, James. But I am just me."

Indeed she was.

As I attuned myself further to the energy around her, I felt like I was opening a door through which entered an incredible warm and beautiful light. Her aura was filled with wonderful energy. First, I saw musical notes dancing in tandem around the top of her head. Each note was a light pastel color. To the right part of her energy field I saw rows of flowers, mostly roses; and the colors were vibrant and alive-looking as if I were standing in a garden and touching them. Around her throat area I saw a luminous violet light blended with a warm blue tint. Whenever I see these colors around the throat center, I know that the person is very creative. I described these visions to Lynda.

"Yes, that makes sense," she said. "I am a music teacher, as well as a voice teacher."

I asked her about the flowers.

"Ever since I was a child I have loved flowers. My father was an avid gardener, and he taught me how to appreciate nature. I learned a lot about flowers and trees from him. I am particularly fond of old roses and have many rare rose plants in my garden. I think what I love best is to stand in the garden with my eyes closed and savor the scents. I just get bombarded with an unbelievable burst of sweet and spice. Every morning I sit in my garden and meditate. You might say that nature fills my soul."

"Well, you are a beautiful person on the inside as well as the outside. The light and color around you is incredible. You seem to attract vibrant colors."

"I'm glad to hear you say that," Lynda said, smiling. "I just started a painting, and haven't been able to decide which color palette to use."

I once again looked at her energy field, which filled

me with its warmth and light. "I don't think you will have any trouble choosing the right colors."

It was at this point that I noticed the spirit of a man standing behind her. He was wearing a plaid shirt and had light blond hair.

"Lynda, there is a man here who says you are his daughter. He is saying the word 'blossom.' This man is calling *you* Blossom."

Lynda's shrieked in delight. Her eyes opened wide, and she whispered like a little girl, "That would be Daddy. He used to call me that because I would pick off the old dead blossoms from the flowers. I thought they were too pretty to throw away, so I would collect them. So he nicknamed me Blossom."

I continued to read for Lynda and was grateful for the spiritual lift she provided the rest of my day. Each of us has the opportunity to become a source of positive reinforcement for the planet. When your aura is a beacon of love, it becomes a force field with the ability to transform the energy of any person with whom you come into contact.

THE AURA OF LIFE

The reading with Lynda and her love of nature shows that each person has an ability to communicate with all living things: flowers, plants, trees, minerals, and animals. One of the ways to develop sensitivity to the unseen is to develop an appreciation of nature. We can all start with the plants in our own homes. I can tell immediately, from a plant's high-pitched cry, that it has been left thirsty or is diseased. Talking to houseplants or garden flowers may seem silly, but it helps us develop a rapport with nature and an appreciation of life on all levels. Each tree and every flower has its unique aura. I suggest to my students that they try to perceive the aura of a flower, starting with its color. Eventually one may be able to perceive the various grids, vapors, and shapes around the flower and its leaves.

The same is true of trees. Trees are especially wonderful to be around because they are very ancient beings, and their auras are full of negative ions, much like water. These negative ions help us to feel recharged, rejuvenated, and refreshed. I remember the time I was in Northern California at a conference. I was feeling rather blue that day and decided to take a ride to one of the giant redwood forests in the area. I felt humbled in the presence of those magnificent trees. I went over and put my arms as far as I could around one of the redwood trunks, and hugged it for all it was worth. Immediately my melancholy faded away. It was as if I had just stepped out of a refreshing shower. I thanked the tree for sharing its love with me and went back to the conference feeling completely recharged.

Trees are constantly communicating with one another. A tree even senses when it will be cut down or destroyed. The vibratory frequency around such a tree will begin to slow down and eventually withdraw. I can illustrate this with an anecdote about a trip I took up the Northwest coast to visit a friend in Seattle. As I drove through the great forests of the land, I was so inspired I started to sing. Then suddenly there was a shift in the energy. I began to pass mile after mile of three-foot tree stumps. It was like being in a giant graveyard; the feeling of sadness was intense, and I no longer had the strength to sing. I got the sense that these trees had been needlessly and callously chopped down. Off in the distance, I could hear the cries of other trees mourning the loss of their loved ones. It sounded very much like the wails of grieving humans.

The earth has its own aura, as do the stars and planets. Think of each living thing interconnected and interrelated, each a transmitter of cosmic frequencies. The weather, especially electrical storms, is our planet's way of transmuting certain energies in and out of its aura. If we look with our spiritual eyes at the big picture of life, we will come to understand that even natural disasters are a way of transmuting energy.

Every living thing plays a part in the evolution of the planet. The build-up of slow frequencies around our planet are made by our own negative emotional outpourings of greed, anger, hate, cruelty, and pain. This is where we humans come into the picture, all too often. We can turn things around, however, and enhance the aura of our planet by emissions of kindness, peacefulness, and love.

Ultimately, it is important that you become aware of your aura, because other people are and they know intuitively if it is strong or weak. When you become aware of your thoughts and actions, you can change

negative aspects into light-filled ones, thus enhancing
the vibrations within you, your home, and our planet.
You can build up such radiance that people will naturally be attracted to you. Your mere presence can heal
someone else. I would love to see everyone's aura
become a shining shield of God Force energy glowing
with the goodness that is inherent in us all.

chapter 4

SIGNALS FROM SPIRIT

*Various Methods Spirits Use
to Contact Us*

After the success of my first book, *Talking to Heaven,* I was invited to appear on *The Oprah Winfrey Show.* Oprah appeared quite perplexed about the nature of communication with the other side. She wanted to know why spirits could not clearly state their names and any pertinent information instead of my having to hear some random thoughts or see pictures.

My response to her was pretty much what I tell other people. First of all, we must realize that there are other levels of consciousness. This means that other dimensions and expressions of life exist beyond the physical one. The time-space ratio and other laws of physics may not apply to these other dimensions—they may be ruled by a system unknown to us. Therefore, spirits won't necessarily communicate in ways that we expect or are accustomed to.

As I told Oprah, "Spirit communication is like speaking a foreign language. Images have unchanging meanings attached to them, whereas names do not." For instance, the names Jodie or White mean nothing because they are merely letters combined to make a sound. However, a car or a house has a meaning attached to it that is clear to anyone, no matter what language he or she speaks.

This doesn't mean that the interpretation of the images is always correct. Often, mediums misinterpret the pictures. For instance, a spirit tries to convey something to me about a necklace she is wearing. She fingers the locket attached to the gold chain around her neck. I may see her touching her throat but not see the locket. I interpret the picture as "something is the matter with her throat," which would be erroneous. Let's take another symbol like clouds. I may see dark clouds and think "bad news," or white clouds and decide it means happiness. However, clouds may signify something else to the spirit, such as confusion. We must bear in mind that misinterpretation or misidentification of the images does not mean that we are not communicating with the spirit world. It means that we are not understanding the message correctly.

Furthermore, the spiritual landscape is *thought*. Therefore, spirits communicate to us through telepathic thoughts. As a mental medium, I "read" these thoughts as feelings, visions, and auditory impulses. I am able to interpret these messages through a common energy that permeates and transcends all levels of existence. I identify it as the God Force energy. Others call it prana. For lack of better words, this energy is love. Love is the ingredient that makes the communication on both ends strong and successful.

One must also realize that someone who has recently passed on is now in a completely unfamiliar world. A spirit may be a bit confused at first because the physical laws to which it had become accustomed no longer exist. Once a spirit recognizes that it is not *dead,* but very much alive—more alive than ever before—it learns that it lives in a world of thought. Thus a spirit must begin to understand how to use thought to create what it wants.

Once acclimated to their new world, spirits begin to hear our thoughts of grief, sadness, and regret. They see the pain and anguish brought on by their death. Knowing that they are still alive, albeit in another form, they want to reassure us that they are still aware of everything taking place on earth. This is not easy, because most of us are so overwhelmed with loss that the last thing we can think about is spirit communication.

Depending upon a spirit's personality, abilities, and its own awareness, it will attempt in every way possible to communicate and get us to understand its newly relocated existence. I have often said at my workshops, "It's like they are playing spirit charades. Spirits are jumping up and down all around us frustratingly trying to communicate a message. And we just don't get it."

Another thing to understand is that a spirit can only draw upon a medium's own life experiences to communicate with that medium. In other words, my experiences become its reference tool. Since I can't tell the difference between a carburetor and a spark plug, it would be difficult for me to understand a spirit describing the inner workings of a car engine.

It is also necessary to remember that spirits communicate from a dimension that vibrates at a faster frequency than ours, and they tend to send their impressions more rapidly than what we are used to on earth. It's as if we are communicating across a vast chasm without the help of a simultaneous translator. It takes a lot of energy on both sides to converse with one another. That is why mediums must stay as focused as possible on the information a spirit is conveying. Often, mediums speak very quickly because they are trying to keep up with a spirit's rapid-fire messages. Over the years, I have learned to emphasize to spirits the need for accuracy in communication. I am constantly conveying to spirits that they must speak clearly and send the message as powerfully as they can.

People often ask, "Why do spirits say such trivial things? Why don't they tell us about the important meanings of life?" Spirits, like humans, have personalities, and use trivialities such as appearance, certain achievements, or even minor incidents to identify themselves. They convey trivial messages for their specificity, so that their loved ones will recognize them as "the real thing." Second, although spirits have an expanded consciousness on the other side, and are able to see every thought and action of their lifetime, their souls are still evolving. Until a soul reaches the higher heavens, its knowledge of life is still limited. Also, spirits will not interfere with our earthly lessons, either as individuals or as an entire planet of people. They will not hinder our spiritual growth by giving us the answers when it is our responsibility to make the correct choices for ourselves.

MENTAL PHENOMENA

So how do spirits manifest their presence to us? Depending upon its ingenuity with manipulating energy and electromagnetic fields, there are many ways a spirit can pierce the dense energy of this slow-moving world called earth. It takes quite a lot of power to finesse these energetic patterns. As I said, spirits primarily use thought to get messages to us. Some of the more common mental means of communicating have been touched upon: clairvoyance, clairaudience, and clairsentience. Other types of mental transmissions are dreams, inspirational thought, automatic writing, and the Ouija board.

Dreams

The sun was so bright that I had to squint. As I acclimated my eyes to the glaring light, I found that I was in a garden surrounded by roses, lilacs, daffodils, and lilies. The air was so thick with floral scents that when I took a deep breath, I could nearly taste these delicious aromas. Every place I gazed, the colors were brilliant. It was a treat for my senses. I started to head straight for the grove of enormous oak trees that bordered the property. Beyond the trees were several cottages with thatched roofs of golden straw and pearl-colored stone. Each one had a charm all its own.

"James, come over here," called a female voice.

The voice was familiar to me, but I had to rack my

brains to recall its exact origin. I turned to my left, walked several steps, and under a very old oak tree stood a woman. She was someone that I had known but hadn't seen in several years. When she turned her face toward me, I was bathed in the delight of recognition. It was my beloved grandmother, Ethel.

"Come on, don't dawdle," she insisted. "I want to show you another view of my house and garden." In that instant, all the years apart seemed to vanish. It was as if we hadn't missed a single beat together.

Grandma looked beautiful in her yellow polka-dot dress. She kept waving her arms, sharing in my excitement. I felt totally complete, alive, and happy.

Then suddenly that feeling came to an abrupt end when I realized that my grandmother had been dead for fifteen years. The blaring drone of my alarm clock broke the silence of sleep. I shot up in bed and peered around the room. The colorful flowers had been replaced by the sight of my clothes, carelessly tossed on the chair, a dresser, and the TV. I was far from the beautiful garden and even farther away from my grandmother. Yet seeing her had seemed so real. Could I have been there?

Practically all of us have had a similar experience "dreaming" about someone who has passed over into the spirit world. I used to call these experiences dreams, but I think they are more than that, because the feelings we experience in them are very real. I now refer to these moments as *crossovers*. Every time I poll an audience, 95 percent say that they have experienced some sort of dream recognition or crossover from the other side. The other 5 percent probably have them also but might not recall them consciously.

People have asked me, "Why do spirits come in our dreams?" And, "Why can't they come when I am awake?" My answer is usually the same. Spirits come in our dreams for two reasons: To reassure us that they have survived physical death, and to let us know that they are a part of our lives and still love us. Perhaps they choose to enter our dream state because we are not in a rational mind-set and, therefore, are more accepting of their visit as a reality rather than as merely our wishful thinking. I often tell people who are unsure of their crossover visit to think about the dream. Did the spirit seem alive? Did the spirit appear as you remembered him or her? What was the spirit doing or saying? If the actions match the personality of a loved one, then it was probably that person.

Besides using dreams to show that they still exist, spirits also use dreams to send us messages. Perhaps they are trying to help us get out of a bad situation or providing us with the answer to some problem that we are having at work.

The main characteristics of dreams are symbols, and it is important that we learn to understand these symbols. There are many books, and even more workshops and classes, about dream interpretation. However, we must understand that not all symbols mean the same thing to all people. A person living in New York City may feel more comforted by the sights and sounds of a busy city than by the stillness of a quiet countryside. For that reason, a country setting might represent loneliness to one person and tranquillity to another. Not everyone's symbolic vocabulary is the same; only you will know what a symbol means to you.

There are many types of dreams besides the typical symbolic dream. Clairvoyant dreams involve seeing visions that subsequently prove to be true. For instance, the other night I had a dream about an ornate building. The next day, as I drove to an appointment, I passed the same building that I had seen in my dream. I had never seen it before. When I talk about dreams in my workshops, someone inevitably comes to me at the end and shares a clairvoyant dream. One fellow said he dreamed of a friend he hadn't seen in ten years. "A few days later I saw my friend's name in the newspaper."

Prophetic dreams are usually about events that come to pass several days, weeks, or even years later. These dreams are rare for most people. However, there are some psychics who can predict earthquakes and other phenomena based on prophetic dreams.

Spirit guides, animal guides, and angels all use our dream state to send us messages. I have a friend whose dreams contain a variety of animals—mountain lions, bears, and alligators.

"Why do I always dream about animals?" she once asked.

"They are temporary spirit guides," I replied. "Their message pertains to the particular experience you are going through at the time of the dream."

I told her to look up the animal in an encyclopedia—its message probably had to do with the characteristics of that particular species. For instance, a bear hibernates. My friend is prone to staying alone quite a bit, so maybe it was informing her that she was hibernating too much.

Having someone with whom you can discuss your dreams is probably the best incentive for remembering and recording them. You can also send a message to one another via your dreams. Pick an image and concentrate on it the night you plan to send the dream message. If your friend receives the same image in his or her dream that night, you will know that your psychic communication was successful.

Dream interpretation takes persistence and attention, but once you learn to remember quite a bit of your dreams, you will be on your way to intensifying your psychic awareness.

Inspirational Thought

Inspiration means "in spirit." For a moment, think back to all the times you were driving a car, watching a television show, cooking, or bathing when, without warning, you thought about someone who had passed on. Or you came up with a solution to a certain situation. You later realized that if you hadn't followed through with your thoughts, you would have suffered some dire consequences. You might say that you were *inspired* to take action.

In this dimension, we rely on the limitations of the physical senses to communicate. But in our natural state of being, which is spirit, we communicate telepathically, by thought. When you pass into spirit, you no longer need vocal cords to transmit words, because your thoughts are immediately received by other individuals. Spirits make contact by imposing their thoughts into our consciousness. It's how they communicate. I like to call it spirit-to-spirit or mind-to-mind communication.

A good way to make yourself open to inspiration is to rest your mind. Get comfortable and take a few deep breaths. You can do this first thing in the morning or at the end of the day before you go to sleep. As you follow the rhythm of your breath, bring yourself to your center, where all is calm. As you quiet the mind, let thoughts pass through. Try not to hold on to or analyze any thoughts; just let them go. Then, when you are ready, open your eyes and jot down each new thought in a notebook. By meditating and quieting your mind, you have opened the channel to spirit, and it will be that much easier for inspiration to come through. I have used a similar process in grief therapy. Writing is a tool that will free the mind to express itself. Expressing your thoughts in a letter to a deceased loved one helps you release pent-up emotions of sadness, anger, forgiveness, or love.

Spirits are around us during much of our waking state, attempting to use thought to influence us to make the correct choices. Many times clients will say that before arriving for their appointments—either in the car on the way over or several days prior to our meeting—they somehow felt a spirit with them. Many people also become aware of spirit energy in times of distress. People will tell me, "I felt I was not alone." They declare that some unseen force or guardian angel was by their side.

We are inspired and encouraged by spirit every day and in every way. We need only be open to clearing our channels for transmission.

Automatic Writing

The intent of automatic writing is different from inspirational thought and stream-of-consciousness writing. Automatic writing happens when the spirit world actually presses us to convey its communication through written messages. One of the more famous psychics known for this type of interface with spirit was the renowned journalist and author Ruth Montgomery. Every morning at nine, she sat at her desk in front of her typewriter waiting for her guides to come through with their messages. At first this was a spontaneous occurrence, but as she explains in her books, this automatic-writing session became a permanent appointment with spirit. We are lucky to be the recipients of the abundance of information that she has brought through.

My first attempt at automatic writing occurred while I was working a nine-to-five job in Los Angeles, on my way to becoming a screenwriter. My day was spent, hours on end, filing papers in the basement of an office building. I remember quite vividly the time I was mentally motivated to find a pad and write something down. Perhaps my mind was already in an altered state due to the repetitious and tedious nature of my work.

At that moment, I assumed that inspiration had struck, and I was ready to jot down an ingenious idea about a script I wanted to write.

I sat with my eyes closed and tried not to control my hand. At first, my fingers felt light and airy, as though they weren't even touching the paper. Then my hand began to move in circular motions. I knew that I was filling the page with circles. The longer I kept my hand on the page, the faster the circles came. Later I learned that this was spirit's method of aligning with my energy field and building up the energy in order to write.

After a few minutes of circles, I began to write letters and words. Because my eyes were closed, I could not make out what I had written. At that moment I wasn't meant to know. I just had to be in a receptive space and let spirit take over. When I felt as though the spirit energy had left, I opened my eyes and looked down at the many sheets I had filled with scribble. All that appeared were circles, some darker than others. I supposed a heavy hand upon the page had made them. On some of the pages, letters replaced circles, but I could not decipher these hieroglyphics.

The first several times I practiced automatic writing, I could not make anything out. The primary results consisted of strange pencil marks on pieces of paper. Eventually, painstakingly, I was able to comprehend one letter and then another. Over time, the letters turned into legible words and I could decipher more clearly the messages being sent. One that I recall was from a woman spirit who called herself Morning Star. I recorded the following passage, some of which is quite beautiful:

> I am close to you in ways of the heart and
> soul. Through you and with you we will
> touch many. As a messenger of peace you
> will share with others the mysteries of life
> and death. For you have had this privilege
> for many existences in the distant land you
> call earth. Your excitement will catch on,
> and together we will reawaken the hearts to
> the truth of the ages. The walls of darkness
> and ignorance will come down, for no
> longer can humans live in fear and
> falsehood. They will open just as flowers
> reach toward the sun. This is the peace I
> leave with you today.
>   Blessings, Morning Star

I had no idea what that message meant for many years to come.

I continued to practice automatic writing sporadically, and different guides, teachers, and spirits made themselves known. Feelings of love, understanding, and joy were always apparent when they entered my space to communicate in this manner. I was never frightened or upset in any way.

The messages continued throughout the following year. They were about human prejudice, our responsibility to nature, the power of prayer and right thinking, my spiritual path, the places I would inevitably travel to, and ultimately the words I would use to teach and help others.

Ouija Board

Before my attempt at automatic writing, I began using the Ouija board, which one might say is another form of automatic writing. Instead of pen and paper, you use a board imprinted with the alphabet, numbers 0 to 9, and the words Yes and No. By placing your fingers lightly on a pointing device known as a planchette, you can begin receiving answers to your questions, spelled out letter by letter.

The Ouija board was one of the first instruments I used in my introduction to the world of spirit. There have been many fears and misconceptions that the Ouija board is a tool of evil. As always, when you delve into the world of the unknown, you must be cautious and properly prepare yourself to attract only the highest order of spirits. If you have a consciousness of fear and hate, you can be susceptible to the unwholesome energies and entities of the universe.

I always began the process of using the Ouija board within a consciousness of love. I would sit for several minutes and meditate to ground myself and raise my energy level. Then I would say a prayer for spiritual guidance, protection, and light. Before making any attempt to contact spirit with the Ouija board, always make sure to surround yourself with love. Then, if you feel a spirit has arrived to communicate, ask if the spirit is from the light. If it is not, it will usually depart.

One of my favorite experiences with the Ouija board happened when I was with my friend Drew. We had been friends for quite a while, and although he had seen me at several public demonstrations, he didn't know that I had also used the Ouija board to contact the other side.

We were at our friend Kelly's house, and her Ouija board was out in plain view, so I decided to show Drew how it was used. After I said a prayer, Kelly and I placed our fingers on the planchette, and immediately it started flying from one letter to another. We took turns asking questions, and Kelly received several messages from her mother.

Then Drew took her place. A woman who identified herself as Mary greeted us.

Drew said, "Mary is my deceased grandmother's name."

After giving Drew many messages of love, she closed by saying, "My son has a good heart."

Drew thought that her message about his father was very sweet. We all knew Drew's dad to be a very kind man.

The next week Drew called me from his parents' house. "I just took my father to the hospital. He has some kind of viral infection in his heart."

The next few days were touch and go, as Drew explained that he came close to losing his dad. However, it wasn't until Drew's last remark that the true meaning of the Ouija board's message became clear.

"The doctors feel he will pull through. They say it is because *he has a good heart.*"

PHYSICAL PHENOMENA

When physical phenomena are being used as a means, a message is projected through the use of material objects and the environment. This type of physical contact includes changes in room temperature, electrical occurrences, rapping and knocking, electronic voice phenomena, spirit lights, telephone and television communication, apparitions, materialization, spirit photography, trance mediumship, transfiguration and apports.

How does this occur? In physical phenomena, electromagnetic energy fields around us are rearranged either through our own conscious or unconscious efforts, or through a spirit's control. Under certain conditions, spirits are able to move the physical objects with which they come into contact. Usually this happens spontaneously. The power and force of these occurrences increase in an atmosphere where people are serious about spirit contact. The following are various methods of spirit communication using physical objects or the environment.

Temperature Change

Most of us, if not all, know what it's like to have goose bumps. Frequently clients will tell me that they were standing in a bedroom or dining room and suddenly felt a chill—often a signal that a spirit is nearby. Another way a spirit will notify us of its presence is through a sudden, spontaneous change in a room's temperature. Many times, while I am meditating prior to a reading, or even in front of hundreds of people in a workshop, I will feel breezes around me and I am aware that several spirits are lining up to convey messages.

Electrical Occurrences

One of the most common signals from spirits attempting to get through is the flickering of lights. Somehow spirits are able to manipulate various electrical impulses. For instance, a spirit will cause a lightbulb to go on and off or even burn out. This always happens when you are around so that you will notice.

This happened repeatedly to my friend Bryan. He would often sit at his desk in the evenings to use the computer. Next to his desk is an end table with a lamp and a picture of his deceased father. Once in a while, the light in the lamp would go off and then turn back on. At first, Bryan didn't think anything of it. He even changed the lightbulb several times. In fact, he replaced the lamp to make sure that there wasn't a short in the wiring. However, the phenomenon persisted. When all the logical reasons were addressed, Bryan realized that it might well be his deceased father trying to get his attention. He noticed that the activity usually occurred on a special occasion such as a birthday or the anniversary of his father's passing.

The first time I appeared on the NBC television show *The Other Side,* I did a reading for a woman named Barbara Matthews. During the show I was successful in bringing through many details about her son, who had passed away. She understood the messages and validated their accuracy. Several months later I visited Barbara at her house.

She told me, "I think I am receiving messages from my son."

I asked, "How? In your dreams?"

"No," she responded. "He is turning the streetlight on and off."

I thought, This I've got to see.

We walked out the front door, and on the corner was a typical streetlamp. We quieted ourselves, and I said a short prayer.

Barbara and I waited in anticipation.

"How often do you do this?" I asked.

"Only on certain occasions," she responded.

Suddenly the light flickered.

"He does three for yes and two for no," she explained.

"What do you mean?"

"When the answer is yes, the light flickers on and off three times. When it's no, it goes on and off twice."

We stood there watching the lamp flicker. Barbara would ask something, and the light, as if sending Morse code, responded.

I asked her, "How long have you been doing this?"

"For the past few months. Usually, when there is some sort of crisis or important choice, I come out here and ask my son."

Rapping and Knocking

Table rapping and knocking is another common occurrence in the context of psychic phenomena. Once when I was back east at my sister's for Christmas, we were all seated around the dining-room table ready to eat a sumptuous feast. As usual, we were talking and laughing and telling stories about our past Christmases together. All of a sudden, we started to hear a tapping noise on the wall. I remember everyone turning around to see if there was someone there. Then the taps grew a bit louder. My sister got up to see if there was anyone in the other room. We stopped eating and waited. I think I said, "Maybe we should say a prayer." We held hands and said a prayer of thanksgiving for the wonderful family meal and being all together at this time of year. Then out of nowhere I felt a cool breeze across my face, and the knocks began again. This time on the window. Again someone got up to look, but no one was there. Right after these last knocks, a picture of my grandmother and grandfather fell off the shelf. I knew right away who was knocking. I said, "I guess Grandma and Grandpa are here after all."

Electronic Voice Phenomena

Spirits can be ingenious in their efforts to be recognized. They can even impress sounds and voices upon magnetic tape. It seems as though the spirit can even manipulate static on the radio. There have been thousands of cases noted by the American Association of

Electronic Voice Phenomena. Some of the sounds are audible, while others only can be recorded on extremely sensitive material. When I sat in my development circle, I experienced some form of this phenomenon. Over a period of months, when we played back our tapes, we could hear audible whispers pierce the silence of our meditation.

Spirit Lights

I define spirit lights as luminous matter. They appear as dots, balls, or gauzy strips of light and range in color from white, yellow, and orange to blue or even violet. The colors may change upon observation, and the lights will flash quickly in the atmosphere. Many people have told me that they can see these lights minutes before falling asleep or when they are in deep meditation. These spheres of light appear off to the side of a person's vision and are sometimes accompanied by a humming sound. During our development circles we would see many sparks of light around the room.

I remember one particular situation at a séance at Brian Hurst's home. Brian had invited me to sit with a group of mediums from Scole, England. This group had been sitting for a little over three years in England, and they had a reputation among paranormal upper echelons of producing some incredible phenomena.

I arrived at seven o'clock in the evening, along with twenty others. We gathered in the living room, and the man in charge of the group explained to us what we could expect to experience that night. During his instructions I tiptoed out of the room and went to the garage where the séance was to be held. I wanted to make sure that everything was aboveboard.

It is unfortunate that so many in this field are not what they appear to be. Over the years I have worked responsibly and honestly, sharing my psychic talents with others. I feel an obligation to expose any person trying to deceive the public concerning spiritualism and psychic phenomena.

I began to inspect every chair, behind the curtains, and even under the carpet for hidden microphones, wires, or props of any kind. I was relieved to find none, but I still felt skeptical.

The group began to enter the garage and take their seats. After several minutes two mediums sat down in front. One of the participants tied their wrists to the chairs with some sort of glow-in-the-dark rope so that we could observe their hands once the lights were turned off.

We opened the séance with a prayer, and took turns expressing our excitement at being there. Brian had turned the radio on to the classical station to help build the energy inside the room. He had also hung immense tubes from the ceiling. The lights were turned off, and we sat for fifteen or twenty minutes in a darkened garage.

At first, the air was still. Then, unexpectedly, it began to stir with movement. The tubes began to chime in rhythm to the music coming from the radio, each one making its own distinctive sound. It seemed impossible, and I was amazed.

Then people began to feel a cold breeze encircle their legs.

"Did you feel that?" asked a woman on my left. "It came right up my leg."

My eyes were glued to the front of the room where the mediums were strapped in the chairs. As people whispered their feelings to one another, several taps, then knocks, were heard above us and on either side of the room.

The two mediums had not budged.

Simultaneously, throughout the room, people began to voice their encounters.

"Oh, my God, someone just touched my shoulder!" was the comment from a man somewhere to my left.

"Look up there. Did you see it?" A woman cried out. She was referring to the flash of light that appeared in one corner of the room.

However, I kept my eyes on the mediums. They were still seated in the same position.

Then, in a matter of seconds, little lights of orange, yellow, blue, and violet filled the air around us.

"How beautiful," said one woman. Everyone seemed mystified.

The lights seemed to grow brighter and traveled around the atmosphere. The more delighted the crowd, the brighter the lights. When people laughed, the lights appeared even larger and brighter. Soon the lights were dancing in the space above us, seemingly leaping from one person to another. At some point a bright yellow orb passed in front of me and stopped.

"Wow, James, it likes you," I heard a man say. I didn't

know if it was Brian. My eyes became transfixed on the light hovering in front of me.

"I wonder if it is someone I know," I commented.

The light began to dance in front of me and seemed to form a smile. Wow, isn't that wild? I thought.

"It is doing that, James, because you don't believe. It wants you to believe," said one of the mediums from England.

Everyone started to laugh because they all knew I was a medium. I was a bit embarrassed, but any doubts I had that evening quickly vanished.

Telephone

Another common phenomenon is the use of phones and answering machines by spirits. The phone will actually ring, and on the other end, you can hear the sound of a voice, often quite faint, accompanied by a lot of static.

The closest experience I had with this phenomenon was the day after Princess Diana died. I was in New Orleans at a conference. It was Sunday morning, and I had the TV in my hotel room tuned to CNN. Like everyone else, I was glued to the set watching the details of the tragedy. I couldn't believe it. I was listening to a report of how the car entered the tunnel followed by another vehicle filled with paparazzi when all of a sudden the jarring sound of the phone made me jump. Usually hearing a phone is no big deal, except that this one rang with the distinctive sound of a British telephone. "Brring-brring . . . Brring-brring . . ."

I looked down at the phone and picked it up slowly.

"Hello? Hello? Is somebody there?" I asked.

There was no response. I put the phone back down, and seconds later it rang again. "Brring-brring . . . Brring-brring . . ."

I picked it up again and shouted, "Hello? Is anyone there, please?" Again nothing.

Then I thought it might be the front desk alerting me to a message. I picked up the phone and dialed. "Did you just ring me with a message?"

"No, Mr. Van Praagh. No one has rung your phone all morning."

"Does your service have the British ring, you know, Brring-brring . . . Brring-brring . . . ? "

"No, Mr. Van Praagh. The phones have American rings. That is the way they have been operating for the past sixty years."

I was flabbergasted as I put the receiver down. *I know what I heard.*

"Brring-brring . . . Brring-brring . . ."

Once again I jumped at the sound of the ring. I picked up the phone and listened. I could hear the sound of someone breathing. Then the phone went dead.

What's going on? I thought. At that moment, I turned my head and saw a picture of Princess Diana on the TV screen. I felt tingling all over. Was it you?

I know it was some spirit trying to get in contact. Because of the uncommon British phone ring, I feel it must have been someone from the British Isles, but I'll never really know if it was the princess.

Television

Several people have told me that they have received psychic messages via the television. This is rare, but possible. One can either see an image of a loved one on the screen when the TV is off, or an image of a photograph when it is on. I have not experienced this phenomenon personally.

However, last week as I packed for a trip in my bedroom, I heard a noise in my living room. No one was in the house except me, so it seemed weird. I walked into the living room, and the television was on. It had turned on by itself. I knew it had to be spirit. I thought, Someone wants me to pay attention to what's on. But at that moment I didn't want to know and didn't have the time to sit and watch. I knew that if it was important, I would find out sooner or later.

The answer came to me the next day. I realized that it was the anniversary of my mother's death, and the program that was playing when the TV mysteriously turned itself on was *Jeopardy*. It was my mother's favorite show.

Apparitions

Apparitions are phantom forms of people and animals, commonly known as ghosts. What is a ghost? A ghost is usually a recently departed spirit that has not yet adjusted to its new life on the other side. Thoughts of the deceased are projected outwardly and usually connect with loved ones, causing the living to, in essence, see the dead. Apparitions seem to move through solid material, to open doors or windows, and even to cause objects to fall off shelves. These souls are desperately trying to get the message of their existence across the dimensions. They often appear and disappear in an instant.

It is also common for the dying to see apparitions a few days before they pass on, as if being called to the other side by those already there.

However, some discarnate spirits can appear to total strangers as semisolid beings. Again one can only say that these souls are extremely attached to the physical plane, and they will linger in its atmosphere indefinitely.

Materialization

Materialization is the process by which solid material is created by the vital force of the members of a development group. A gauzelike, colorless and odorless substance known as ectoplasm will emerge from the ears, nose, mouth, or solar plexus area of the medium and form into "physical" matter. This can be a disembodied spirit or parts of a spirit. The spirit will possess all the properties and appearances of a physical body, and often will seem to have solid flesh and bones.

Ectoplasm is extremely sensitive and almost impossible to manifest in normal light. That is why physical mediums usually work in a dark environment. There are very few physical mediums on the earth today. I had the rare opportunity to participate in this phenomenon on a trip to Brazil, and I will describe my experience in Chapter Five under the heading "The House on the Hill."

Spirit Photography

Spirit photography is a phenomenon whereby spirit bodies appear on photographs and began around the late 1800s with the advent of spiritualism in the United States. Although much of it is disputed and often fraudulent, there is no denying that many spirit images have been and continue to be impressed upon photographs.

Part of the explanation lies in the camera itself, as it is apparent that a camera is far more sensitive to light waves than is the human eye. The photographic plate can detect things that we simply cannot see. It is therefore understandable that the camera can pick up the energy bodies of spirits that are invisible to us.

As we have discussed throughout the chapter, if a spirit is able to manipulate energy in such a way as to disclose its existence, anything is possible. Here again a spirit may use the energy of the living—in this case, the photographer-medium—as a link to project its energy onto the photographic film. A spirit picture is usually taken against a dark background. In the development process, spirit photographers magnetize the photo with their vital energy force by touching it.

You do not have to be a skilled photographer to induce this phenomenon. If this type of psychic connection is appealing to you, and you are sensitive, persevering, and patient, you can obtain such photographs.

A friend of mine, Joerdie Fisher, is an excellent medium, and much of her mediumship is working with photography. Often when she takes a photo, streaks of energy can be seen around the subject. On occasion, faces of departed loved ones appear in the photograph next to the subject.

Aura photography is another popular phenomenon, which reproduces the electromagnetic waves around the subject's body. These waves emanate from the etheric body, or etheric double, not the physical body. When the photograph is developed, you can actually see blots of colors around the subject, red, green, blue, and yellow being the most common colors.

Trance Mediumship

Trance mediums are able to slow their brain waves to reach a deep level of relaxation. A trance state can be induced by meditation or hypnosis, and trance mediumship can be achieved only after extensive study. Depending on the medium, there are various degrees of a trance state, from light to very deep. When a medium is in this altered state, a guide or spirit will blend with his consciousness. Often the medium's voice pattern will change as the guide or spirit speaks through him. The same is true for a medium's handwriting when a spirit communicates through the written word. Channeling is similar to trance mediumship.

Transfiguration

In transfiguration, a spirit imposes its face upon the face of a medium. For instance, a young female medium will take on the features of an old man—this superimposed image will be consistent with his appearance as he looked on earth. Transfiguration is not limited to human beings. Animal spirits have also appeared in this way.

Apports

Apports are material objects that literally appear out of thin air in a séance room. Many times they are small objects like jewels, stones, or flowers. The theory behind this phenomenon is that the object comes from the fourth dimension. Often an object will dematerialize in one part of the world and materialize in a séance room in another part of the world.

Signals from spirit may be elaborate or simple, but they are always around us. We need only to become sensitive to understand their meaning. When you are working with the invisible realms, remember that there is always a higher intelligence in charge. Not everything that you desire can be achieved because you want it to. We are here to live as best we can with integrity and responsibility. Within this framework it is possible to succeed in contacting the spirit world. Don't be discouraged. Certain things will be easier for you than others. Concentrate on developing those abilities that are natural and appropriate for you.

chapter 5

ANGELS AMONG US

*Meeting and Working With
Spirit Guides*

When I was eight years old, I experienced my first encounter with an angel. I was lying in bed when a cold gust of wind blew across my face. Just then, I looked up and saw a large, glowing hand above my head. I wasn't afraid—somehow I knew that this was a benevolent sign. For me, this hand represented peace and protection. I called it the hand of God, and thought of it as my guardian angel. I knew it would always be with me, and whenever I felt alone or unhappy, the hand of God, my guardian angel, would be there to lift me up.

Growing up Catholic, I was taught from an early age about guardian angels. I always felt comforted in knowing my guardian angel was by my side. The concept that angels interface between heaven and earth has been around for as long as recorded history. Reports of religious occurrences having to do with spirit beings, angels, and prophetic signs have all had universal acceptance at some time.

Today bookstores are filled with books about angels and angelic encounters, and television shows and movies portray the interaction between humans and the angelic worlds. For the past several years there has been a wonderfully successful TV series called *Touched by an Angel*. It has been so well received by the general public that it is now in syndication around the globe. Why does this show work? I think it demonstrates the goodness that each soul is capable of possessing, which makes the series appealing. More important, people are drawn to the angels.

We may think of angels as fictional creatures, but angels are real, even if we cannot prove their existence in human terms. If you believe in them, you are in very good company. Some of the people who have believed in these celestial beings are Emanuel Swedenborg, Dante, Thomas A. Edison, W. B. Yeats, J. Paul Getty, and Jesus. Many people believe that angels walk among us on this earth, the way they do on the television show. They may not have wings, but their hearts are as pure as gold.

The word angel derives from the Greek word *ange-los,* meaning messenger. Angels are often viewed as the personification of God's will and are depicted with wings to signify their celestial origins. We know these angels as the heavenly host or the court of the Most High. Along with our guardian angels, there are a variety of angels that guard us, heal us, and minister to many different needs in the universe. They have been divided into nine orders: seraphim, cherubim, thrones, dominations, virtues, powers, principalities, archangels, and angels. There are also elemental spirits—devas, fairies, gnomes, and elves—that act as angels to the plant kingdom, and they watch over all of nature.

Angels evolve in the spirit realms side by side with humans. Most of the time, we are unaware of their presence because we are so caught up in our physical lives. The good thing is that we do not have to be conscious of their closeness to be blessed by their beneficial work. The angelic hierarchy shows by example how to live in joy, creativity, and spontaneity. Its function is to praise the glory of the universe and all that dwells within. These beings will take any form necessary to help people in distress. I believe that angels operate in very similar ways to spirit guides, and often I perceive them as one and the same. We never know from day to day who is around, watching and inspiring us from a spiritual land.

The more we become aware of angels, guides, saints, ancestors, and loved ones in heaven, the more we can use their assistance on earth. Through contact with such angelic beings, we learn that we are always connected to our own divine wisdom.

AN ANGEL IN DISGUISE

Part of the reason I find this work so special is that I can see very clearly how individuals learn to accept their lives. There have been occasions when the information coming through one of my sessions is unexpected, and may not become clear until many days or even months after our meeting together. Miracles do exist, yet we rarely know who may be pulling the strings on our behalf.

Let me give an example. I was doing a lecture in San Francisco, and I was drawn to someone in the crowd. "Excuse me," I said, pointing to a brown-haired, middle-aged man sitting in the third to the last row of the auditorium. "I would like to come to you."

People craned their necks to see the person sitting in the back of the room.

"Me?" The man stood up, holding his finger at his chest.

"Yes. I see a huge fire truck behind you with its lights blazing. Do you understand this?"

He nodded. "Yeah, I do. I'm a fireman."

The crowd laughed.

"Oh, well, that makes sense, then," I joked. "There is a man in front of the truck, and now he is moving next to you. He is wearing a fireman's uniform."

"Yeah, I get it. Go on."

"Who is Carl? Do you understand this name?"

"That's my name," the fireman responded.

"This spirit man in the uniform gives me the name of Ed or Eddie."

Carl shook his head and put his hands to his eyes. I didn't hear a response.

"Do you understand this?" I asked.

"Yes. Ed was my buddy. We worked at the same station house together. I can't believe it. Eddie, man, I am sorry. Could you please tell Ed I am sorry?"

"You can tell him yourself. He can hear your thoughts."

I continued communicating Ed's message to his buddy. "He wants me to tell you to stop beating yourself up. It wasn't your fault. It just happened."

Carl knew what I meant. He started to cry.

At that moment a beautiful spirit lady with golden hair came into view. She floated gracefully like a ballet dancer. She whispered into my left ear.

"Do you know Chestnut Street?" I asked Carl.

Carl looked dumbfounded. I could see by his expression that, as far as he was concerned, this remark came from left field. After a beat, he could barely contain himself. "That was the street my family lived on when I was a boy."

"I have a blond lady standing here, and she is telling me that she knew you when you were a boy. She talks about the room in the house with the dominoes."

Carl's face turned white. "Ah . . . ah . . . I get it. When I was a boy, I used to play dominoes in my room. I would set up patterns, and . . ." His voice trailed off.

"Yes? Is there something else you would like to say?"

"No one knows about that. How do you know?" He was skeptical and wanted some sort of confirmation.

"This lady was there. She is telling me that you saw her," I said.

At that moment, Carl sat down in his seat. I think he was in shock, but I could not let his reaction disturb me. I had to concentrate on the information coming through spirit. "She is telling me about the snake. Do you remember?"

Angels Among Us

Carl sat bewildered, attempting to recall his past. Finally he let out a sigh. "Oh, my God. Who is she? Please tell me who she is."

"She is giving me the name of Loretta. Do you understand this name?"

"Yes. Loretta is my mother's name, but she is still alive."

"Well this lady with the blond hair has a connection with your mother. I am not sure what it is. She shows me a P, as in Patricia or Patty. Please ask your mother who this connection would be."

The reading went on for just a short while longer. At the end, the blond-haired spirit spoke about a warehouse.

"She is telling me about a food warehouse. Do you understand this reference?"

"Oh, my God. I don't believe it. That's where Eddie died," Carl admitted. He explained to the crowd that he and Eddie were at a three-alarm fire in the downtown warehouse district. They were soaking the top floor when it gave way unexpectedly. Eddie was holding on to Carl for dear life.

"I tried to hoist him up, but he kept pulling me down. Then the whole floor crumbled beneath him. That's when Eddie fell. I thought I was going to die next. Then I felt this incredible peace come over me, and I saw a blond-haired woman giving me her hand. She had an angelic face. She reminded me of someone I had seen before. Then I blacked out."

When Carl came to, he was in the hospital. The other firefighters told him that he was found on the opposite side of the room far away from the collapsed floor. He never told anyone, not even his wife, about the vision he had that day. "I always thought of her as my guardian angel," Carl said. Then he admitted, "She was the same vision I had seen as a boy playing dominoes in my bedroom. Back then, I used to think of her as my imaginary playmate. I would leave the room, and find the dominoes completely rearranged when I returned." He had never mentioned this blond woman to anyone, and he seemed relieved to share it with an audience that perhaps was empathetic with him.

Several months later Carl called my office, insisting on speaking with me. "Tell him it's the fireman with the blond angel," he said to my assistant.

I picked up the phone. I wasn't ready for what he was about to say.

"James, remember that blond lady that came to me?"

"Yes, of course. Did you ask your mother who she is?"

"Yes, that is why I am calling you. First, I want to thank you."

"You're welcome," I replied.

"You gave me my life back. You really did. I asked my mother if she knew a blond woman with a name starting with a P, possibly Pat or Patricia. My mother seemed irritated at first. She wanted to know why I was asking. After some coaxing, she finally told me the whole story. The blond-haired woman was my natural mother. Her name was Pat. She died from a hemorrhage when she was pregnant a second time. My father met my mom soon after, and they decided not to tell me about my birth mother," Carl explained.

"Unbelievable!" I said in amazement.

"It was my mother, James, who saved my life. She really was my guardian angel."

"And she still is and always will be," I responded.

"It's good to know I have her on my side," Carl said.

Here was a man truly grateful for the recognition of an angel in disguise.

SPIRIT GUIDES

Like angels, spirit guides are highly evolved beings that are a source of energy and expertise to us. Guides, like angels, are always learning and maturing. Working with us on earth is part of their inter-dimensional training— they will attach themselves to us to learn a particular experience so they can progress as guides. You might say it is a two-way proposition. Guides help us to learn and to grow, and we help them to improve their skills as guides.

There are a variety of spirit guides that come in and out of our lives during the course of a lifetime. Some of them have walked upon this earth as spiritual teachers, leaders, and saints, while others may have never touched its surface. Jesus, Buddha, Saint Francis of Assisi, and other saints and avatars are but a few of the illumined beings that have inhabited the earth plane. These are master beings that brought growth and spiritual development to soul groups. Although they no longer serve as personal guides, a consciousness evolved from their teachings remains on earth. Some call this the Christ Consciousness or the Cosmic Christ, and there is always someone on earth whose destiny is to uphold this Christed awareness.

The primary function of a spirit guide is to help, protect, assist, and inspire you in your spiritual evolution. People have asked me many times, "Do we all have a spirit guide?" The answer is yes. We have many.

Spirit guides come to us in many forms, including members of our family and friends who have passed over and continue to protect and watch over us. Guides will usually appear to us dressed in ways that are easily recognizable. For instance, a guide will wear either the robes of a monk or the garments of an American Indian, depending on our beliefs. This ability to resemble a variety of figures and expressions is used by guides to gain our trust.

The most important thing to understand is that guides are always aware of our needs—even if we are not. Just like a teacher, a guide can show us the way and inspire us to make the right choices. However, it is always up to us to decide whether or not to follow our guide's direction. The following are but a few of the main spirit guides that come to us during an earthly lifetime.

Master Guide

This particular being, who is involved in our everyday spiritual growth and wisdom, has been with us throughout our many incarnations and continues to teach us the lessons that are necessary for our spiritual evolution. You might think of this guide as part of your soul family—you and your master guide agreed to work together prior to your incarnating. Often you will be aware of this teacher as someone who keeps coming into your consciousness, especially in your dreams. You will feel a great affinity for this guide, as if you were a part of him or her.

The job of a master guide is to inspire, guide, and teach us, as well as help direct us toward our destiny on earth. This guide remains with us during the interim states of existence when we return to spirit.

Gatekeeper, or Protector Guide

This being's main role is to protect your space from any energies that might cause you harm or any entities that might take possession of you. This guide is particularly important in mediumship because of the multitude of spirit energies that bombard a medium's electromagnetic field. This guide also protects you when you go out of the body or into a trance state during meditation or at a development circle. Protector guides also assist us when greater strength or courage is needed.

Inspirational Guide

These guides assist us in learning a myriad of soul lessons like compassion, purity, patience, understanding, unconditional love, forgiveness, spirituality, and creativity. Sometimes these guides are with us for a brief period of time, until a certain skill is developed.

Such was the situation when a spirit came through by the name of André. I was attending a séance given by world-renowned medium Lesley Flynt, and I was totally surprised by the outcome.

During the séance, André told the group that he once lived as an artist in France. He said that he would remain close by me and help to develop my sensitivity as a medium, adding, "In several years this man will become well known because of his work in aiding the masses. He will write a book that will reach the minds of many. We are helping you, my friend, in this quest. You are not alone."

André reminded the group, "The spirit world is always involved in your earthly lives, decisions, and choices. Nothing in the spiritual realms can hurt you as long as you approach your work with discrimination and common sense. If a spirit tries to control you, you must recognize the behavior and dismiss the spirit from your life."

Helper Guide

These beings are drawn to us through the universal law of affinity: Like attracts like. We attract what we need or want to learn according to our interests. For instance, if you want to sculpt a statue, you will attract a helper guide that has expertise in artistic creativity. This also holds true for other inclinations. Writers will draw beings with writing expertise that inspire them in their endeavors. Scientists will ultimately draw guides that have an understanding of their particular areas of investigation.

Relationship Guide

Relationship guides can include friends and members of your family that have your spiritual evolution at heart. The love bond that was created on earth continues to exist in heaven. This type of guide will inspire you to make choices for your highest good. I believe that this spirit being assists us greatly by creating relationship scenarios in our lives from which we can learn and grow. Our spiritual development comes first, and is of the utmost importance to our guides. Whoever will help us to have a more complete understanding of life will be sent our way. No one is in your life by mistake.

Healing Guide, or Spirit Doctor

A healing guide is a being that is fully involved with our health. At times this guide will inspire you to take better care of your physical well-being and will work with universal forces to assist in the correct alignment of your energy fields. Whenever you go through physical distress or illness, your healing guide will work on fusing healing cosmic energies into your force field.

These healing guides, or spirit doctors, at one time might have been healers or doctors on earth. Not until very recently was I aware of this particular type of guide, as you will see from the following episode.

THE HOUSE ON THE HILL

On a trip to Brazil I had an extraordinary opportunity to meet and collaborate with other mediums. I was invited to a healing center outside Rio de Janeiro. A German monk known as Freiz Luiz founded this center more than thirty years ago as an orphanage. As time went by, it evolved into a medical facility for underprivileged children. In its present incarnation it is home to two hundred mediums who are also licensed doctors and medical practitioners. They work exclusively with the most desperately ill children of the country.

One of our discussions was about spirit guides. Several of the mediums told me about their contact with spirit doctors. I was told that these spirits have chosen to return to earth to help the human population and that certain spirits felt guilty about making wrong decisions on earth and wanted to return so that they could make amends and free themselves of karmic obligations. In addition, many spirit doctors return to assist people in areas of the world where doctors are needed.

On the last Saturday of the month, the weakest children are brought to a place known as the House on the Hill. It is a small house used exclusively for the manifestation of physical mediumship—its energy is devoted to manifesting spirit in physical form.

Physical mediumship is extremely rare, and I was especially interested in seeing it firsthand. The wonderful people at the center were glad to let me witness this phenomenon, provided I conform to certain disciplines prior to attendance. The rules were clear: no eating red meat, no drinking alcohol or taking drugs, and no sexual relations for forty-eight hours prior to the sitting. This abstinence regimen is to safeguard the physical energy of those present and to ensure that everyone's energy is strong enough for the manifestation to occur.

At five o'clock in the evening, I was escorted up the hill. I was given a locker and asked to change into an all-cotton top and pair of pants, similar to the scrubs a surgeon wears in a hospital operating room. After changing, I was led into a reception area furnished with several lounge chairs. I was told to wait there and to pray. As I closed my eyes in meditation, I could hear lovely angelic music filtering through the speakers into the room. The melodies helped lift my spirit and got me into the proper attunement for what was about to take place.

After two hours I and several others were led by flashlight into another room practically devoid of light. After my eyes adjusted to the darkness, I could see that the room resembled a small theater. All two hundred seats were filled. A very faint blue light shone upon a raised stage in front of us. There were five beds on the stage situated side by side as in a hospital ward.

One of the members of the congregation came onto the stage and, in Portuguese, asked everyone to recite a few prayers after him. The medium was already seated in a cabinet on the stage. The room became still, and one by one, five small children were brought up and laid in the beds. By now my eyes had adjusted to the darkness, and I could see clearly what was happening. I did not want to miss a thing, as this was a once-in-a-lifetime opportunity.

Watching carefully, I noticed a small wispy cloud take shape in the center of the stage. The cloud continued to grow very slowly. It seemed as if hours had passed by as the energy continued to build and the substance eventually turned into the shape of a man. This shadowy spirit was dressed in scrubs right down to a surgical mask and latex gloves. He was holding a rod that looked like a conductor's baton and began moving from bed to bed pointing the rod, which emitted colored lights, at the children's bodies. He worked extremely quickly using this mysterious rod. It took about five minutes to get through the five beds. These children were taken away, and five more children took their place. This continued for at least a half hour. I was overwhelmed by a simultaneous sense of wonder and gratitude.

Then something occurred that I will never forget for as long as I live. Two assistants walked up the aisle, stopped, and raised their flashlights, toward my face. I knew they wanted me to go up onstage. I could feel my whole body shaking with the energy of spirit as I followed them.

I lay down on one of the beds, not sure of what to do or what to expect. I kept very still. After a few moments the masked spirit, whose name I later learned was Dr. Fritz, appeared next to me. I looked up at his face and noticed his deep-set, peaceful, yet penetrating green eyes. He pointed the lighted baton at my abdomen. Lying there, I knew that I was seeing a physical manifestation of a spirit, and I would not have forgiven myself if I didn't at least attempt to touch it. So I brushed my arm on the side of Dr. Fritz's leg, and I felt his solid physical form.

The following afternoon, I went to lunch with one of the administrators of the healing center. She said that she had been talking with the elders about last night's experience on the hill. "They want me to thank you for coming. Because of the high vibration of your energy, you made it possible for us to work on twice as many children as we normally do. We will be forever in your debt, as you will be in our prayers."

I also learned that the spirit, Dr. Fritz, had particularly wanted me to come onstage for a healing. No one at the center had any idea that at the time I was having ulcer problems, which have since gone away.

The experience in Brazil was so magical and enlightening that I often think about it when I am doing demonstrations. I am grateful to the spirit doctor for healing me on so many levels. I believe that the spirit world had given me an enormous gift of insight into the incredible power of spirit's involvement on earth.

LIVING GUIDES

The deceased are not the only ones who are our teachers or guides. Often in life, we encounter people who come onto our path to direct and guide us. I have had many of these guides, but the most memorable of all is a woman I spoke about extensively in *Talking to Heaven*. Her name is Connie Leif. When I was very young, Connie taught me the invaluable lesson of how to believe in myself. She bolstered my self-confidence and told me that I would make it in the world. Without this confidence I don't know if I would have had the fortitude I obviously need to do the work I am doing.

I also believe certain friends and acquaintances are part of our lives as teachers. They help us by giving us a perspective that is usually different from ours. Friends will also see the best in us and stay with us during both good and bad times. There are friends who may come into your life for a short period of time, make their mark, and then leave. They, too, are guides. We just have to take the time to recognize them.

RILEY

Many people have asked me if animals can act as our guides and protectors, and I always answer with a resounding *yes!* As I have said many times, animals are the greatest teachers of unconditional love. A wonderful example of just such an animal angel happened during a reading several years back.

Erica Burlingame was in her mid-thirties. She wanted to reach her father, who had passed into spirit several years earlier. Immediately at the start of the reading, her father appeared.

"Your father is speaking to me about wintertime,"

I said. "He is showing me a pond. I don't understand what that means, but this is the image he is showing me."

Erica thought about that image for a few minutes and then said, "Yes, I understand. Go on."

"He is talking about a time when you were eight years old. I don't know why he is mentioning this."

Suddenly another spirit came through, which completely changed the feeling of the reading. "Your father is talking about Riley. He has Riley with him, and Riley wants to be known to you."

Erica began to cry.

As soon as her eyes began to tear, I saw a huge Irish setter jump on her lap and give her a lick. "There is a dog here giving you a kiss!" I said with a surprise.

Erica nodded, taking a tissue out of her purse. She was obviously moved and emotionally overwrought. She tried to tell me something but couldn't quite get it out. "He . . . he . . . save . . ." she mumbled.

We waited a few minutes so that she could get hold of herself. Once she calmed down, she spoke. "Riley was my dad's dog. When I was a little girl, he would follow me around and wouldn't let me go anywhere on my own. It was strange. My family usually went ice-skating at the local park. One day I skated away from everyone and fell through some thin ice. The last thing I remember was my dad calling my name. The next thing I knew I was in a hospital bed looking up at my parents. They told me that Riley saw me fall in and was able to grab my collar. He waited there with my jacket between his teeth until Dad was able to pull me out.

Riley saved my life. From then on I considered Riley my best friend."

I particularly felt blessed to be in the presence of this great animal protector. The reading continued for some time. At the very end, Erica summed up her gratitude. "Thanks, James. You brought through two of my guardian angels. I couldn't have asked for anything more."

CONTACTING YOUR
SPIRIT GUIDES

In order to establish and build a relationship with your spirit guides, you first have to become receptive to them, and ultimately be able to feel and see them. You can do this by reserving a space in your home where you practice spiritual work daily. This spiritual work is different from the work you do in a development circle. In a development circle you are working to build the energies of the group, whereas in spiritual work your contact with spirit guides has to do with personal spiritual progress. Make sure the space you choose promotes relaxation and inner harmony. You must have no distractions. Reserve this time for you and your guides.

The next step is to put yourself in a relaxed state. Close your eyes and take several deep breaths. After you are relaxed and the mind chatter quiets down, begin to go through the *preliminary groundwork* that I describe in Chapter Nine.

Once you are in proper attunement with the energy

waves vibrating up and down your spine, you will begin to feel an energy egg or aura around you. It is important that you become familiar with your energy field.

The next part of this meditation is very important. As you keep the rate of your breath consistent and the grounding cords in place, imagine a beautiful place where you want to interface with your guide. It might be by a cascading waterfall, in a field of flowers, or on the top of a mountain. Use your imagination with as much intent as possible. This area will become your meeting place. This is where you will come to talk and work with your teachers and guides.

Once you are in this place of serenity, use your thoughts to ask your master guide to stand in front of you so that you can see him or her. Once you see your guide, ask questions: Who are you? How do you work with me? What is it that you want to teach or reveal to me? Is there a particular message you have? How do you relate to me? What is your mission for me?

Notice your guide's physical traits, such as eye color, hair color, clothing, and anything else memorable. Your guide may have personality traits that seem unfamiliar to you. Accept what you receive without judgment. Focus on love.

When the time is right, ask your guide to respond to you. Then listen. Pay close attention to all of your senses. Realize that your guide may answer visually or audibly. The answer may be a spark of light, a whisper, or a whole dissertation. You may detect a scent in the air around you in response to your inquiry. Be prepared to feel your auric field change as you align with your guide. Notice how your guide attunes to you and your energy field.

If you feel several guides in your energy field, ask them to identify themselves either by name or a symbol. Again, ask them about their purpose, mission, and what they want to teach you.

As you work with your thoughts and meditation, you will feel more confident and will be able to draw your guides closer to you.

Once you have performed this exercise several times, you will begin to become aware of the influence of your guides. The more you access their wisdom, the more you thrive in their light-filled energy, and the easier it becomes for your psychic senses to open to the spirit realms.

TESTING YOUR GUIDES

Once you have established a comfortable rapport with your guides, it is time to verify and validate their messages. Be aware that some guides may not be as highly evolved as you expect. It is important that you know whether you are in contact with your spirit guides, with another entity, or simply with your own imagination, so you must test them. You will know through the vibrations you feel whether the guide is positive and suitable for you.

As you test, ask for specific information about yourself or a particular situation with which you are dealing. In the succeeding days or weeks you will be able to validate your answers one way or another. If you find the information inaccurate, try again, perhaps several times. Sometimes it may be a matter of misunderstanding or misinterpreting the message.

For example, ask for a particular sign that lets you know your guide is nearby. Ask that it be simple to recognize, perhaps something like a purple flower. In the next couple of weeks if you receive a flower from someone, or if something happens involving a purple flower, you will have confirmation. If after some time no validation is given, you need to go within once again and reestablish the connection.

Another way to test your guide is to seek answers or messages for other family members and friends that can then be validated. Always do this with the utmost respect for all parties concerned, and with the intention that this information is to gain trust in working with your guide, and not for you to gossip.

I must advise you that sometimes the messages you receive may not be joyful ones. You may receive disturbing information. If you are ready to ask it, you must also be ready to receive it. Keep in mind that you can misinterpret the message. This happens more times than not. Just make sure that you stay true to yourself and your intentions.

If for some reason you sense that your guide is not coming from a compassionate place, then you must reestablish your center through your *preliminary groundwork* exercise, release this being, and send it back to its own space. At this early stage of development, I advise

you to refrain from trance mediumship. You do not
want to let an entity take over your consciousness. I
will explain more about this in the next chapter.

ETHERIC GUIDES

Before incarnating to earth, we discuss our soul's
growth with a group of highly evolved beings known
as the Etheric Council. This is the way we decide on
what we want to learn, our purpose in life, and the
karmic debts we want to balance. When we incarnate,
our master guide stands by and makes sure we follow
through on these decisions.

During the second year of my development as a
medium, I became aware of several of my guides all at
once. This happened in the wee hours of the morning. I was in sort of a twilight state where I was neither fully awake nor actually asleep. I remember distinctly evaluating what had transpired in my sleep
because I knew that I had been traveling outside my
body. I thought, I want to go back to where I just
came from, and instantly I found myself in an incredible, majestic hall. The sides of the building had dia-
mond and gold arches that ascended toward the heavens. It reminded me of a magnificent cathedral. The
walls gleamed with the brilliant hues of blue and violet. I had an overwhelming sense that I was in a center
of learning.

In front of me was a long library table made of
a translucent material. The assemblage of materials

seemed to be blended in perfect harmony. Scattered throughout the chambers were plush gold-cushioned chairs. Here people read or conversed with one another in a scholarly manner. Bookshelves lined the walls behind the plump silken chairs. As I scanned the rows, I noticed that each book was like a living, breathing energy in its own perfect place, organized according to its subject matter.

At that moment, I realized I was in the Hall of Reflection, where spirits learn, expand, and develop their mental capacities, and receive instruction from *their* spirit guides and teachers.

Suddenly a golden-haired man appeared in front of me. He was wearing an ethereal taupe-colored robe with gold trim. He seemed ageless. I felt a rush of warmth as I peered into his gentle eyes, sparkling with sea-blue love. I had seen him before. Then I realized that he was one of my teachers. He spoke to me telepathically. "Please sit. You have one more lesson to understand."

He gestured to several other people sitting around the table, each one distinct from the other. There was a woman with straight brown hair, an impish face, and flushed cheeks. For some reason I knew her name was Elizabeth and that she was involved in human psychology. My gaze shifted to two other men. The first was dark-skinned with a rather gaunt but wise face and a bright smile. The other appeared a bit older and more serious. He wore wire-rimmed glasses. I knew he was involved with something to do with chemistry or alchemy. He bowed his head toward me and smiled in approval. I was suddenly filled with pride, as if I had completed a job well done.

These were my spiritual guides. They had lived on earth, but probably a very long time ago. They seemed removed from anything of an earthly nature. As I sat there, they questioned me telepathically and then answered those questions, so that I could fully comprehend the many layers of meaning. No one spoke, for no lips moved. Although these were four distinct individuals, they communicated with one collective thought. "You must be patient, James. The time has not matured for your project to enrich you, and in turn to serve others."

I felt deep down that I had to learn patience for all things to happen in their proper time. I knew then that everything in life happens in the time allocated for it. I realized that it was no use wasting energy worrying about end results. It would only distract me from living day to day and enjoying my life.

I recognized that I was looking into the faces of some of the teachers in my Etheric Council. This was the team of guides that watched over me and impressed me with acceptance, patience, knowledge, self-belief, discipline, compassion, joy, and humor. These were the divine forces that kept me true to spirit and out of harm's way.

I opened my eyes and stared at the ceiling. I knew that I had been with these spirits, because it felt extremely real. I knew that I would see them again, and I have, on many occasions.

Some people think that you must *see* or *hear* your

guides to know that they are there. However, you can just as easily *sense* or *feel* their presence. To do this, you must stay in a higher vibratory rate. The best way to keep your energy high is to love yourself as you would love your own child. Have faith in your abilities and trust the universe to give you the answers.

chapter 6

PSYCHIC PROTECTION

Psychic Vampires, Astral Entities,
and Other Potentially Harmful Energies

Once you have learned the many ways to open up to psychic contact, you are bound to interact with a variety of energies, spirits, and even thought forms—some that may not be for the highest good. Any occult activity undertaken without knowledge and care can open dangerous doorways to powerful forces. You must learn how to be mindful and fully in control of your own space before entering the psychic arena. I often tell students that having awareness and knowledge is not enough. You must be vigilant in safeguarding yourself from energies that are potentially negative or harmful.

Please realize that the spiritual and material worlds are not separate from one another. The astral level that is within and around us is a meeting place for many influences that originate in the physical, emotional, and mental activity of human beings. These elements are not always beneficial and can be detrimental to our well-being.

In addition, our own fears, anger, depression, and desires can invite unwanted energies to invade our psyche. Guilt, especially, is a harbinger of bad influences. If we consistently do things out of guilt, we unconsciously condemn ourselves. Guilt and punishment go hand in hand and undermine our spiritual center. If we have done anything that we continually feel ashamed of or guilty about, we need to find compassion and forgive ourselves. Otherwise, we unwittingly deplete our own energy supply. When we become spiritually and emotionally drained, we become exceedingly sensitive to external energies and vulnerable to unwanted psychic vibrations.

Sexual intimacy is another way that people can open themselves to psychic attack. We must learn to use care and common sense in our relationships with others. The more we love and respect ourselves, the healthier and happier we become, and the higher the vibrations we attract on a daily basis.

NEGATIVE THOUGHT FORMS

Have you ever walked into a room or building and moments later felt uneasy? You sense heaviness in the atmosphere or experience a sudden onset of goose bumps. What is going on? The intuitive self is picking up certain vibrations, or thought forms. Thought forms are energies that still inhabit a space, having occupied it for many years, decades, or even centuries. These vibrations can be violent and foreboding, or peaceful and benevolent.

Most of us have visited an old cathedral or church, and upon entering sensed a feeling of reverence and serenity. The energy was probably subdued, almost hushed from years of loving, God-like thoughts in the form of prayers and songs filling the space. Positive thought forms thrive in this kind of environment—just as negative thought forms thrive in a place where people are persecuted or full of rage, like a prison.

As you can well imagine, I am quite sensitive to my surroundings. I can be flying over a city and sense a shift in the energies from one place to another. Some people might think this is wonderful, but it has its ups and downs.

A few years ago I went on a lecture tour through the Greek islands with Dr. Brian Weiss, author of insightful books such as *Many Lives, Many Masters*. The experience was breathtaking and filled with life-transforming experiences. Many of our ports of call were ancient towns filled with historical richness. I felt that I was stepping back in time to lands of legend and magic that one can only imagine.

However, my feelings of warm rapport changed when we disembarked at Istanbul. For some reason, when I got off the ship and walked to the center of the city, I was overwhelmed by an unbelievable amount of stagnant energy. I had a difficult time catching my breath and felt as if I were suffocating. As we walked through the streets, these bad feelings worsened. I made several comments to Brian and the other passengers that, "something doesn't seem right here."

As I discovered the city's history from our tour guide, I realized the cause of my negative reaction. Istanbul, the former Constantinople, is the site of some of the worst massacres in human history. It was said that the country's flag, which is a crescent moon and a star upon a red background, represents an observation made by Sultan Murad I in A.D. 1389. While wandering the killing fields of a recent victory, he saw a bright star and the crescent-shaped moon reflected in a pool of blood. That bit of information validated my intense reaction. I was sensing centuries-old thought forms of hatred and upheaval that lingered in the atmosphere.

THE RED BRICK BUILDING

Being highly sensitive, I am susceptible to feelings of sadness, depression, and anxiety. This was what I felt in Istanbul. There are often times when I can't wait to leave a certain place. I had such an experience on yet another trip.

About three years ago, I was presenting a workshop in Alaska and on my way there, I had to spend the evening in Vancouver, Canada. Several members of my party and I were walking down a main street on our way to a restaurant for dinner. All of a sudden, I stopped dead in my tracks.

"Wait a minute, you guys," I said. "Something is wrong here. I can't go any further." I had begun to experience terrible cramps in my stomach and a burning sensation around my right ear. At one point, I thought I was going to throw up. "I have to cross the street," I said to my puzzled guests.

Quickly everyone helped me across the street and sat me down against a building. Once I was off my feet, the feelings of undue depression and anxiousness subsided. I began to check my energy to see what kind of interference I was picking up. At the same time, I knew to protect and ground myself from unseen influences. Assessing my reaction, I realized that I had walked into an area of extremely negative energy.

I looked across the street to a red-brick building about ten stories high. As I gazed up at a row of windows on the top floor, I noticed black bars across them. I could tell some very cruel things occurred behind those windows. I could hear the agonizing screams of those trapped inside.

The eaves of the building featured religious statuary, including a figure of Jesus with his hands outstretched. Then I looked down and read the sign on the front gate. To my surprise, it was a hospital. Nonetheless, I sensed that many people had suffered barbaric and cruel therapies in this place of so-called healing. The hospital was definitely haunted by the many souls that died needlessly within its walls.

As I looked at the red-brick building, I could feel the pain, anger, fear, and hate of the poor souls seeping out. These ghosts continued to roam the hospital corridors reliving over and over the agony caused by shock therapy and other strange experiments. Because they could not attain awareness and consciousness, because they scarcely knew where they were, these spirits were truly trapped.

Their souls remained earthbound because of a lifetime of fear. This, and more, I could sense in the atmosphere.

I explained my feelings to my friends, and they agreed that the building seemed to have a dark cloud around it.

Just recently I was again in Vancouver to do a lecture. I was riding back to the hotel with a friend, and on our way, my friend suddenly pointed out the window. "Wow, check that out," he said. "It looks like something out of an old horror movie."

I looked out the window and once again came face to face with the eerie red-brick building.

I took a deep breath and thought, If you only knew.

A GRASSY KNOLL

As you can see, I often have many psychic encounters when I travel. One of my incredible experiences occurred in Dallas during my book tour for *Talking to Heaven*. I had just finished an interview downtown with a local Dallas newspaper. My media escort, Marie, ushered me out of the building and on to the next interview. As we drove along one of the main thoroughfares of the city, I suddenly felt quite peculiar.

"Please stop the car," I said.

Marie pulled over and turned off the engine.

"Something feels odd to me. The energy suddenly feels very intense."

I looked around the area and knew I had seen the place before. "Where are we?" I asked her.

Marie knew all too well what I was referring to. She answered rather awkwardly, "We are a block away from the book depository from which President Kennedy was shot."

I could feel the blood rush from my face. I had thought about visiting the site of the assassination while in Dallas but knew my busy schedule would probably not permit it. "I'd like to get out and walk down to the next block."

As soon as I got out of the car, I centered myself and said a prayer. Then silently I performed my protection ritual. As I started to walk toward the area, I began to feel a lot of dense energy. The closer I came to the building, the denser the energy became.

I stopped fifty yards from where Kennedy was slain and felt the panic, the craziness, and the horror. It seemed that particular moment in history was forever frozen in time. Metaphysically speaking, such a fateful event has an everlasting effect. The street may have been repaved and the surrounding area may have been relandscaped, and even the building may have been renovated, but nothing diminished the profound energy of that moment. It is still very much alive and etched into that space for all eternity.

As I assessed the area, I had a clairvoyant vision of what happened that terrible day in Dallas. I do believe that there was a plot at play, and it involved several men. Two in particular were definitely responsible for killing the President—I'm sure of that because I could see two men escape in a car. The door of the car had been altered to make it look like an official vehicle. These two men got away unnoticed and headed to a small municipal airport nearby.

I have not yet had the opportunity to confirm these impressions with the spirit of John F. Kennedy, but one day I hope I will.

LEARNING TO
DETECT THE SIGNS

I sense negative influences through my physical body. Usually I begin to feel sick or strange. However, everyone is different. How would you know if you were around negative psychic energy? The following are some symptoms of psychic attack from negative influences:

- insomnia and sleeping disorders
- recurring nightmares and dreams of terror
- low energy levels in the morning
- feeling zapped or drained around certain people or places
- stomach upset or cramps
- an obsession about a certain person or thing
- anxiety or pressure around certain people or places
- a nervous breakdown
- headaches that occur a few minutes after you talk to a certain person
- chronic headaches
- feeling tired as soon as you enter a certain building, store, or house

- chronic fatigue and exhaustion
- bad or repulsive odors around people or places
- bizarre occurrences
- frequent accidents
- sudden onset of depression or moodiness

THE ROSEANNE SHOW

Every once in a while, even I let down my guard and get overwhelmed by psychic energies that invade my space. I remember the time I was on *The Roseanne Show.* I was near the end of my book tour and was already fatigued. On that particular show I read for several people, and each reading seemed more emotional than the next. By the time I had finished, I was physically and emotionally drained. Upon returning home, I went to see my friend Michael Tamura, a great psychic healer.

Michael looked at me and said, "I can tell that you have been on TV recently. There is a lot of energy around you, and it is *not* yours." He began to describe in detail several of the people for whom I had read two days earlier.

"Oh, my God," I blurted out, "you're exactly right."

Not only had I opened my energy field for spirit contact, but I had also accumulated everyone else's at the same time. All the people for whom I read and anyone else in the studio audience were tied into my energy field. No wonder it felt like I was carrying the weight of the world on my shoulders.

PSYCHIC VAMPIRES

I feel an obligation to explain the seriousness of understanding energy transfer, and how certain people in your life can affect you in a detrimental way. These psychic vampires can siphon off your energy to the point where you are completely debilitated. Many of them vibrate at low frequency levels and attract negative astral entities. When you are around psychic vampires, you can feel this low vibration. You may not know what you are feeling, but intuitively you are aware that something is oppressive, depressing, or unstable.

When people project anger, rage, jealousy, hatred, envy, fear, and resentment, they drain your energy. Often they are not aware that their negative energy is extending beyond them and hurting others—they are too wrapped up in their own misery. A person filled with pessimism and denial, always perceiving the dark side of life, discharges low vibrations into the atmosphere. Like ripples on a lake, these vibrations undulate outward and affect everyone and everything within their sphere.

This is also true of someone who is extremely fearful and overwhelmed by doubt and distrust—everything seems gloomy and hopeless. This individual could be anybody—your co-worker, husband, friend, the cashier at the supermarket, or your dentist. Constant fear is an open invitation to astral entities.

It's important to notice when your body feels stagnant or your emotions are out of sorts. Begin to recognize changes in your behavior around certain people and in certain environments. Notice if you always get a headache after you enter a friend's home. Do you become uneasy or upset when you think about meeting a specific individual? Does your mood change when you enter certain buildings? Listen to your intuition and pay attention to signals from your emotional and physical bodies. You cannot isolate yourself from the world—you are a part of it. You can, however, minimize the effects of the negative psychic influences that surround you by becoming aware, conscious, and alert.

TOO CLOSE FOR COMFORT

When Jenny showed up for her reading, she looked as if she was ready for the hospital emergency room. I was struck by the dark cloudy blotches and jagged rips in her aura. Red and black tentacles were attached to her heart chakra, squeezing the life out of her. I could tell that this woman was quite ill and in a lot of distress. Before I could do a reading, I needed to heal some of the pain and disturbance surrounding her energy field.

"What's going on with you?" I asked.

Jenny admitted that she was married to an extremely negative man. "He is ruthless in business and brings all that animosity home with him. We hardly speak anymore."

She confided that she was suffering from chronic fatigue syndrome, systemic candida, and fibromyalgia.

It was very clear to me that her symptoms were directly related to her husband's energy and their failing marriage.

I began to tend to her spiritually, clearing her aura by first sweeping out the debris and smoothing out the tears. Then I was able to raise her vibration.

I knew it was in this woman's best interest for me to be blunt. "I believe that you are under psychic attack," I said. "It is most probably your husband's negative energy. By being close to him and intimate with him, you are exposed to all his ill will. Do you understand the concept of a psychic vampire?"

"I think so," Jenny said.

"Because your husband is dishonest and deceitful, he attracts lower energy forms into his aura, and these lower vibrations will pull on your energy as well."

My frankness struck a chord with Jenny. She realized that she was living a lie and that she had to restore her balance and sanity in order to get well. Soon after our visit she began divorce proceedings.

I left town for several months on an extended tour of workshops in Europe. While I was away, Jenny called my office for another appointment.

When I finally saw Jenny again, I almost didn't recognize her. Her aura had changed completely. The holes and blackness had all but disappeared. She looked happy, healthy, and alive.

"What happened?" I asked in surprise and delight.

"I finally left my husband," she replied. "It wasn't easy. He was mean and hurtful, but I prayed a lot for guidance."

Jenny continued to tell me that within a short period of time after she left him, her symptoms began to disappear. "I started to regain my physical strength and from then on, I was on the road to recovery."

Jenny is now living a life free from pain and depression.

When you are close to someone who is a psychic vampire, sometimes the only alternative is to leave, as Jenny did. If you feel you cannot leave a person—say, an aging mother—then you will need to be vigilant in keeping your aura strong and healthy in order to protect yourself. In Chapter Nine I will give you instructions on how to protect yourself from negative energies. A strong defense is as important as a good offense.

PSYCHIC MANIPULATION

We often attract people who mirror our weak points and negative feelings. A good way to stay free of unwanted psychic influences is to become aware of the thoughts upon which you dwell. Such was the case with my friend Diane. When Diane entered her mid-forties, she started to worry about her looks as she aged. She told me about her experience at a party.

"The host had hired a psychic to read palms for the guests. When I sat with the palm reader, she told me that unless I changed my line of work, I would begin to age very quickly, within a year's time."

Although Diane confided that she really didn't

understand what the reader meant and carried on with her life as usual, she took the stranger's message to heart.

"I could hardly believe it!" she exclaimed. "Within a year of my reading with that psychic, my hair turned gray. I would look in the mirror and notice lines creeping around my eyes and mouth, and the skin under my chin starting to sag."

Diane started to feel anxious because the negative prediction was coming true. "James," she told me, "the words of the palm reader kept spinning around in my mind. I believed her because she was a psychic—I felt she would tell me the truth."

Eventually Diane learned that the palm reader had spread her negativity to other people at the party. In fact, she told everyone something foreboding and worrisome. One person admitted to my friend that he had heard through the grapevine that the palm reader worked with dark forces.

Diane realized that if she continued to believe the negative forecast of the palm reader, her words would become reality. Diane decided to take control of her own thoughts. "Every time I even think of getting old, I say 'Deflect.' I think it's working. I hope so."

Diane's story reminds us that no matter what, no one has power over you. In every circumstance and around any person, you always have the power to say no. You most certainly have the power to say no to negative thoughts and fearful images. It is only when you allow people or situations to take charge of you mentally and emotionally that you open yourself to unwanted, debilitating energies.

ASTRAL ENTITIES

Lower astral entities can intrude on our energy fields when our auras are depleted. As I commented in Chapter Three, when we indulge in negative thoughts and out-of-control behaviors, especially alcohol and drug abuse, we weaken our auric shield and risk invasion. Unevolved entities miss the comforts of the physical world and often want to reexperience them by attaching themselves to the energy fields of the living. Remember that when a person passes into spirit, he retains the same mind-set that he had on earth. So if someone was angry on earth, it is more than likely that he is still that way in spirit until he learns differently.

Entities feed on the negative behavior and emotions of the person they have invaded, and will actually influence him to engage in more negative behavior. Entities will instigate arguments and generate situations that lead to outbursts of anger and rage. It becomes a vicious and dangerous cycle. The more negative you are, the more negativity you create.

Lower astral entities can cause severe psychological impairment, mental and emotional instability, confusion, sudden mood swings, and sudden atypical dysfunctional behavior. Someone affected by lower-entity energy will often display self-destructive patterns and severe mental disorders. Unevolved entities can also hinder the healing process and cause prolonged physical illness, because they need that painful energy to live on.

Entity invasion of a human body is a touchy subject.

Many people identify this phenomenon with extreme cases of obsession, as in the film *The Exorcist*. This only breeds more fear about the invisible worlds around us. But such intrusions can happen in subtler, more stealthy ways—and are much more common in this form.

IF ONLY I LOVED MYSELF

During a visit to San Francisco, where I was conducting a workshop at the Whole Life Expo, I had several appointments, one of which was with a woman named Alissa. For our meeting, Alissa had driven about two hours from a rural town to the home where I was staying. She had been looking forward to her reading for several months. The information that came through my reading for her clearly demonstrated the importance of being cautious about the people with whom we associate.

"I see a young woman here who has your eyes. She actually looks like a younger version of you," I told Alissa.

"Yes, I understand."

"I believe she is your daughter. She tells me she is one of two."

Alissa's eyes opened wide.

"Do you understand the name of Marcy or Marcia?"

"Yes, that's right. Oh, my God, you have my baby. My baby is here," Alissa cried. "Oh, thank God. Is she with her grandfather?"

I sent this thought back to Marcia.

"Your daughter is telling me that she is with someone named Burt and is telling me about going back to school."

"Yes. Burt was a playmate of hers when she was a child. He died when he was very young. He was riding his bicycle and got hit by a car."

"Your daughter tells me that she is happy now and sorry that she caused you so many heartaches when she was in high school."

The mother acknowledged this insight and was anxious for me to continue.

I proceeded to bring through not only her daughter, but also Alissa's father, Montgomery, and a number of other relatives. It wasn't until the end of the reading that the true meaning of this connection was revealed.

"Do you know the name Christy?" I asked.

"What is that name again?" responded Alissa.

"Your daughter is mentioning the name Christy and is telling me to acknowledge her."

I could tell by the look on Alissa's face that she was a bit uncomfortable about Christy. However, Marcia insisted that she needed to speak about her friend Christy.

"Marcia is telling me that she was in a lot of pain. A lot of emotional pain," I explained.

"Yes, she was. Terrible pain."

"Your daughter is talking about not knowing herself. She had a terrible self-image and keeps on talking about her demons and how Christy influenced her."

With this bit of news, Alissa let out a loud cry. "I

know! I know! It wasn't her! I knew it wasn't my daughter. I didn't even know her. She had changed."

"She is telling me that she is sorry that she was not nicer to you. She is trying to convey that she was not strong enough to fight off Christy's energy. She is saying that Christy attracted very negative and bad situations into her life. Christy thrived on drugs, power, and darkness."

Alissa acknowledged these circumstances and explained that Christy had been a heroin user since she was fourteen.

"Do you know the name Sam?" I asked.

Alissa was dumbfounded. She opened her mouth, but nothing came out. Finally after a long minute, she replied. "Sam. Yes, I understand. Oh, honey, I know you didn't mean it. Oh, my God."

I relayed Marcia's agonizing regrets. "I didn't mean to do it, Mom. It wasn't me. You've got to believe it wasn't me. It was Christy. I just did what she wanted me to. I am so sorry."

The reading continued for a short while. I was able to glean from the communication that Marcia and Christy were best friends. Christy was a very negative individual who had psychically drawn to herself very low entities. These astral entities influenced her life and unfortunately also came into Marcia's sphere of energy.

It was at that point that Marcia revealed a gruesome tale of how Christy filled her head with terrible lies about this man named Sam.

"Your daughter is telling me that all she wanted to do was kill Sam for causing her friend pain," I explained. "She is saying that her thoughts were not her own. She was being used."

Alissa sat in silence as I continued the messages from her tormented daughter.

Through the visions that Marcia sent, I could see the gory details of a deadly plot. Marcia showed me how she waited one night behind a bush in front of Sam's apartment. When he arrived home, she took a 45-mm gun from her bag and shoved the weapon to his head. As he rushed to get away, she shot him. Then she turned the gun on herself and pulled the trigger.

"She now knows how wrong it was," I told Alissa, whose face was streaked with tears. "She is now telling me the importance of being true to oneself. She is sorry for being weak and letting Christy take control of her. She is saying that she didn't have the strength to fight her off. Your daughter was not living her own life. She is telling me that she was living out Christy's stuff, not her own. She wished that she loved herself more."

Marcia learned the hard way that in the process of living someone else's life, we can completely and utterly destroy many other lives, including our own.

PROTECTING YOURSELF

The best way to guard against unwanted thought forms, negative energies, and psychic vampires is to strengthen your aura. Envision it as an invisible protective shield of light around you, able to deflect any negative energy that comes into your space. Remember also that you have spiritual helpers in the form of angels and spirit guides that are always ready to assist you.

Here are some of the basic ways to build a strong aura that will help safeguard you from negative energies:

- Get enough restful sleep.
- Pay attention to your dreams.
- Exercise regularly, relax, and eat good food. A weak body is a vulnerable body; a healthy body is the best defense.
- Have a good, loving attitude toward yourself and others, and defuse thoughts of anger, rage, and hatred.
- Stay away from places that contain and attract negative vibrations.
- Avoid hateful, gloomy, angry, and fearful people.
- Spend more time outdoors in nature. This has an enormous positive effect on your electromagnetic energy field.
- Try to keep your personal home and work space reasonably clean and neat. Physical dirt attracts psychic garbage.
- Let go of self-criticism and self-judgment.
- Forgive yourself for everything. Forgive others too.
- Laugh every chance you get. Laughter is sure to break the bonds of negativity.
- Bless the individual who you think is harming you.

- Ask your angels and guides to protect and shield you.
- Most of all, fill yourself with the light of the God Force energy with every breath you take. Ask that only the energy that is for your highest good reside in your body and aura.

Remember, prayer and meditation are the primary means for protecting yourself. As you prepare physically, emotionally, and mentally for spirit contact, you must also learn how to fend off unwanted negative energies. When you strengthen your aura and follow the guidance of your higher self and spiritual guides, you will become discriminating and wise with people, places, and events.

chapter 7

MIRACLES EVERY DAY

*The Extraordinary Experiences of
Ordinary People*

When I first began to explore spiritualism and the paranormal, I researched hundreds of books on the subject, ranging from self-help manuals on meditation and self-empowerment to works on psychic development. As I progressed in my studies, I realized that the books were linked by a common thread—the concept that the power of the mind can generate change.

EXPECT A MIRACLE EVERY DAY

Ever since I read this expression twenty years ago, it has been my credo. I have discovered that miracles are possible if I use my thoughts in positive and beneficial ways. The possibility to manifest what I want is limited only by my thinking.

One day I found myself at a Sunday service in the Hollywood Church of Religious Science. Although I was unfamiliar with its doctrine, I quickly learned that its tenets had resonance with my life. These tenets, drawn up in the 1920s by Dr. Ernest Holmes, included a belief in one divine energy source manifested through all creation. In this worldview, all human beings connect to this universal intelligence through their thoughts and intuition. The minister explained that we are all responsible for our current lives and that our thoughts are at work creating our futures as well. As I listened to these words, I knew that they were the truth for me.

I realized then that life is an extraordinary tapestry. Our needs, wishes, and prayers are carefully woven into this tapestry; with each breath and every step we weave the threads. How we choose to incorporate life's offerings into our tapestry is always up to us. When we open our hearts and minds to the undeniable support of the divine energy at work in every aspect of our lives, miracles do happen. On those occasions when we are in communion with our divine souls, even the simplest acts of creation, like the sun rising in the east or a bird sailing through the sky, testify that every day a miracle is waiting to be born.

WHAT IS A MIRACLE?

Are miracles something we create, or are they unexpected divine gifts that descend from the heavens? Must we pray for a miracle or are miracles given to those who need them? Is a cure for cancer a bigger miracle than the blossoming of a rose?

A miracle is an occurrence that takes place within the natural course of events and transcends physical laws as we know them. A miracle is often associated with a religious belief or a supernatural manifestation, yet it is much more. To a clairvoyant like myself, miracles are steps in a cosmic dance. They are the results of our thoughts coupled with an acceptance of the energies that surround us. I believe miracles are like seeds. When planted and watered by our attention and appreciation, they bloom.

Miracles are an active principle in life. The German mystic Jakob Böhme called this principle "the signature of the spirit." In the Kabbalah, this active or creative principle corresponds to a vortex of spiritual energy in space. The ancient Jewish mystics who studied the Kabbalah called this vortex "kether," meaning crown of life.

So the question arises, do miracles come only to those who believe in God? Do miracles happen to certain people because they are better than others? We do not have to believe in God for a miracle to occur in our lives. God is not a person but an all-encompassing loving force, and that loving energy, that spark of God, resides within each one of us. Everyone has an opportunity for a miracle, but we have to be open to receiving it.

My contact with the heaven worlds might be described as a miracle. To be able to bridge both worlds and be touched by spirit absolutely convinces me of the infinite possibilities available to everyone. Imagine the wonder of being able to glimpse the glory of heaven right here on earth! I have been blessed with miracles many times, and have seen lives forever changed by such occurrences. With each revelation and unique perspective of human life from a spirit's point of view comes an overwhelming sensation of joy. The knowledge that we are truly limitless spiritual beings is too incredible to ignore.

Spirits often speak of the power of God within each individual. How do we recognize this power of God? The quickest way, they assure me is by taking down the walls of self-criticism and self-judgment and nurturing ourselves with *love*. In doing so, we begin to live in the realm of possibilities where miracles reside.

When we have love for ourselves, we begin to live in a state of God-consciousness. This is living in heaven while walking upon the earth. Living from this loving consciousness, we are aware that all things are possible, and we are prepared to take part in the fruits of our spiritual heritage, commonly referred to as miracles.

BE TRUE TO YOURSELF

Many years ago, a client by the name of Joanne came to me for a reading. As spirit presented itself, I learned that Joanne had had a very difficult life. She had been abused as a child and became a runaway. When I saw her, she still seemed to be searching for her true identity.

"I have a woman here with dark hair," I told her.

"She is holding what seems to be a Bible. Do you understand this?"

Joanne hesitated. "I'm not sure."

"She is showing me a picture of a church. Now she is opening the doors and going into it. It is filled with people. They are standing with their hands over their heads. It looks like some sort of church service."

"Oh, of course. Yes. That is my friend Rose. She helped turn my life around when I was living on the street."

"She says she is still watching over you."

Joanne shared her relationship with this spirit. "Rose was like a missionary. She would roam the streets looking for lost souls like me. She found me at the lowest time in my life. She fed me, gave me clothes, and read me stories out of the Bible. If it wasn't for her . . ." She broke down in tears.

I sat quietly waiting for her to gain her composure.

"I became a born-again Christian, and turned my life over to Jesus," Joanne continued. "That was over twenty years ago."

"Rose is saying that you are still searching for answers. She is showing me an easel and a canvas. Do you understand this?" I asked.

Joanne told me that ever since she was a little girl, she had loved to draw and paint. She always felt wonderful and alive when she was painting. "But I never felt I had any real talent. Besides, I had to make a living to support myself," she explained.

I told Joanne, "Start painting again. Rose will be at your side to inspire you."

With the information revealed in her reading, Joanne decided to return to her art.

Years after, I heard about a woman named Joanne from someone in my workshop. This was the same Joanne who had come to me for a reading. I learned that she had become an art therapist and was quite well known in her field. She had obviously followed the advice of her mentor and spirit friend Rose. Today Joanne is helping others find their true selves as she was once helped to find hers.

Everyday experiences, even those that are painful and horrible, like abuse, abandonment, and addictions, have meaning for our souls' development. Just as Joanne was helped by spirit to find her soul's longing and become free from her low self-esteem, we all can learn lessons of commitment, forgiveness, cooperation, and patience. The messages we receive from heaven can help us in the smallest ways, from getting parking spaces to the more important issues of recognizing our true self-worth.

TIMING OF MIRACLES

People are usually eager to know, "When will such and such happen?" My reply often surprises them. "When God says yes, do you say no?" We are so caught up in the quick fix that we often miss the myriad opportunities that come knocking at our door. Miracles happen in spirit's time. That is the truth. When you set the energy in motion with a creative idea, it will manifest in the time deemed proper for your growth. But who knows when that will be? Today, tomorrow, this year, next year, next decade, or next lifetime? The universal laws that govern our souls are very different from those that govern our physical world. In the cosmos there is no such thing as *time* as we know it.

Instead, there is a great rhythm to the energy of life and all creation. Everything flows in and out like the tides. The universe will always have its rise and fall, action and reaction. This is a universal law and is as natural as our breathing in and out. The Hermetic masters understood this law of rhythm and learned how to compensate for the inherent swings of life. By removing themselves from the desires of the ego, and by refusing to give in to negative mental states or emotions, they neutralized the backward swing of the pendulum. In other words, if you want a miracle, expect it to happen. The stronger the intent, and the purer the desire, the faster the energy will move.

LETTING GO

As much as we may try to will things to happen, we must learn to let go and allow spirit to do its part. This doesn't mean that we do nothing. We must move forward with faith and trust in a universe that supplies all our needs and desires, as you will see in the following example.

A woman by the name of Rebecca came to me for a reading several years back, very depressed by her present circumstances. She was out of a job, severely over-weight, and losing her house. She applied to several companies for work, but nothing seemed to be connecting for her.

"I am doing everything possible to get a job, but I feel like I'm up against a brick wall. Can you help me?"

I looked at her aura and saw sparks flying every which way. I knew that she had been struggling to make things happen for a long time. I told her, "I think you need a change of scenery. Sometimes you have to let go and let God, if you know what I mean."

Rebecca seemed puzzled for a moment. Then she said, "Well, I have a sister who lives in the Northwest. Maybe I could stay with her for a while."

The reading commenced, and the spirits that came through encouraged Rebecca to join her sister, where she would find peace of mind.

"But I still don't have a job," she objected, "and my house is in foreclosure. I feel that I should be doing something to correct this situation."

I could tell that Rebecca was stubborn, trying to control life in a way that fit into her belief system. "I understand," I replied. "But I have a feeling that something is waiting for you, if you can trust in your God-self."

As she was leaving, Rebecca hugged me good-bye.

"Please let me hear from you," I said.

Two years later Rebecca called my office. "I have to come and see you in person. I have some news to tell you."

When Rebecca showed up at my door, I was flabbergasted. She had lost about a hundred pounds and looked like a completely different person. "Oh, my God," I said, clasping my mouth.

She just stood there smiling like the Cheshire cat.

"What happened?" I asked.

"I went up to my sister's in Oregon. At first it was very difficult. She wasn't used to living with anyone after her children had moved out of the house. I wasn't used to living with anyone either. So we had to adjust to our new arrangement. I got a job up there at the local health-food store and started using their supplements. I learned a lot about nutrition and fasting. We lived out in the country, so I was able to take long walks in nature. Eventually I started to lose weight and feel better about myself. Then out of the blue, someone called to find out some information about an animation company I once worked for many years ago. A month later this person came to Oregon on a completely unrelated matter. He gave me a call, and we had dinner. During dinner he asked me if I would be interested in being a production coordinator for an animated film his company was financing. Well, I am on my way to Italy. I have a two-year contract, and they are going to provide a tutor so I can learn Italian."

I sat silently in openmouthed wonder.

"You know, James, I once said to myself, someday I want to visit Italy and take a walking tour of Tuscany, but I never had the time or the money, and I was too self-conscious about my weight to even consider it. That was probably ten years ago. Who would have guessed it would happen this way!"

It was apparent to me that Rebecca had to let go of doing things her way so that spirit could grant her request in its way, in its time.

THE ART OF MANIFESTATION

All matter in the physical universe is a manifestation of the mind. Manifestation in the psychic realm is a product of our mind conjoined with the great Universal Mind. Our job is to learn how to tap into the tremendous resource that is within and around us. The universe will give us everything we want, but we must be careful how we design our order. If we go to a restaurant and order chicken, we don't expect to be served steak. The law of affinity guarantees that we will attract to us what we store in our minds. If we want poverty, sickness, or unhappiness, all we need is to focus on these conditions, and we will attract them into our lives. We in fact create these conditions with our thoughts.

People who are motivated by fear (there are a lot of them) view the world upside down. Fear causes limitation and uncertainty, and leads to all sorts of negative situations. When we are fearful, we feel separated and isolated from the world. This diminishes our power. We must stop looking at the world from a "poverty" consciousness. We are the only ones who can turn away the abundance that life has to offer.

How do we manifest a miracle? There are four easy steps.

1. Define your intent.
2. Be specific about what you want.
3. Believe it is true.
4. Live it as if it has already happened.

By backing a thought with the purest intention, that thought is free to exist without the fear or limitation that would only slow down the process. Pure intention does not include judgment or ego, or insist that something manifest itself in a certain way. When you color a thought by the conditions of your ego, you run into trouble because, ultimately, fear enters the picture.

I was speaking to a friend one night about some control freaks we know. Control is another face of fear. When you want to be in control, you are sending a message to the universe that things *must* happen within certain parameters because you believe this is the best way. Your mind may be so intent on wealth that you watch every nickel spent and miss the opportunities that could have earned you millions.

By not letting go, you miss the true gift of the universe. Know that you deserve all that life has to offer and that the universe will *always* provide what you ask for.

I finish every lecture with a series of self-empowering affirmations. One is "Healthy am I, happy am I, holy am I, and so it is." I want people to start thinking and living the rest of their lives from this point of awareness. Every situation in my life is ruled by this affirmation; "I am a full, healthy, happy, and holy individual."

One cannot say these words and, presto! expect it to be so. One must live life consciously, with an awareness that the universe is abundant and fulfilling every wish and desire. If you desire complete health, happiness, and holiness, you must see health, happiness, and holiness everywhere you go—not just when it is convenient to see it. With this mind-set in place, you will draw to you all that makes these conditions *real* in your life.

When we open our minds to the incredible unlimited universe, we become participants in the active flow and infinite energy of life. We begin to live a much larger existence. We become interested in life. As our awareness expands, we learn of the unique and distinct facets of living on this planet that will help to define our hopes and our destinies.

When we use a limited consciousness based on fear and lack, anything out of the ordinary will seem unusual. However, when we are aware of the power and magic of the universe, and life itself, extraordinary occurrences, or miracles, are natural.

YOU GET WHAT YOU ASK FOR

Over the years, many clients have come to me with a desire to find that perfect someone to love. Tammy was one of these people. She would call me often, and eventually we became friends.

Time after time she would say, "I'm so lonely. I just want someone to love. I don't want to be alone."

Tammy had low self-esteem. She had a difficult time

finding something worthwhile to love about herself, never mind loving another.

"Love yourself the way you are right now," I explained, "and you will open the space in your heart to attract someone."

I told Tammy to write down the traits she wanted in this person with whom she hoped to share her life. Besides clarifying her intention, I thought this exercise would force her to take a look at her own good qualities. She never seemed to get around to doing that. As time went by, our lives took different directions and we drifted apart.

Several years later I ran into Tammy in a coffeehouse. "What have you been up to?" I inquired.

She spent the next half hour telling me that she had changed jobs a few times, and that her mother had died and she was grieving her loss. "I'm still looking for someone to love," she added. "I guess the universe forgot about me. I have no one."

"Did you ever write down a description of the person you're looking for?"

"No, I never got around to it. The universe knows what I want."

I explained to her that it takes a little more than that. "You have to know exactly what you want and live in that knowingness."

Tammy just smiled and said, "Well, I guess I will just live with my cat for the rest of my life."

I asked her, "When did you get a cat?"

"Oh, my neighbor moved, and since I really loved the cat, I told her that I would keep him. I love

Whiskers; he's a sweetheart and good company. At least I have someone to share my life with."

At that point I looked her straight in the eye and said, "Your wish has been granted."

"What are you talking about?"

"You told me years ago that all you wanted was someone to love so that you didn't live alone. Guess what? The universe gave you what you wanted."

It was obvious to me that Tammy still hadn't learned to love herself. I explained that animals are great teachers of unconditional love and acceptance. "Perhaps the universe sent you Whiskers to help heal your feelings of fear and self-doubt."

Tammy looked sadly down at the floor. "I guess you're right."

It is not enough to have a desire for something. You must also believe that you will receive it. The clearer the focus, the more accurate the manifestation.

SYNCHRONICITY OR COINCIDENCE?

During a recent lecture in Canada, as part of a discussion on psychic awareness, I asked the audience to pair up and participate in a psychometry exercise. I instructed one partner to hold an object belonging to the other and see what happened. The goal was to learn to use intuition to pick up information about the other person through the energy attached to the object. After five minutes I asked the audience to discuss the impressions they received with their partners. Then I asked them to share their stories with me. A group of four women raised their hands.

One of them stood up and explained, "I think we have something unique to tell. My sister and I paired up with these two women in front of us. They are sisters too. All four of us have a last name that begins with the letter C. Last week we all went to the same cemetery on the same day to visit our grandparents. We found out that we arrived less than two hours after they left. Not only that, but we learned that both sets of grandparents are buried in the same row next to each other. Now, what are the odds of that?"

Was it a coincidence that these four women out of a possible twelve hundred people happened to sit right next to each other? Or was it some cosmic plan at work? Did these women attract each other because of the similarities in their backgrounds? How many "coincidences" happen to you? I, for one, have had enough to know that nothing happens by accident.

The summer I turned eighteen, my high school buddy Scott and I hitchhiked across the United States. When we reached San Francisco, we ate lunch at the famed Fisherman's Wharf, and we noticed four other guys wearing backpacks. We introduced ourselves and learned that they were German tourists on summer vacation like us. They were planning to hitchhike to San Antonio, Texas, the next day. Having passed through Texas on our way west, we shared some helpful directions and road stories. They were grateful for our guidance. As we got ready to leave, we bade our fellow travelers good-bye and good luck.

The following week, on our way back to the East Coast, Scott and I hitched a ride with a couple who dropped us off on a country road somewhere in Arizona. We were several miles from any main highway and totally lost. Scott and I walked up the road to an intersection hoping to find more traffic. Upon our arrival at the intersection, we saw four figures sitting off on the side looking at a map. We wondered who else was stuck in the middle of nowhere. As we got closer, we recognized the four German guys. We let out a sigh of relief. As we greeted each other, our fellow travelers directed us back to the main highway.

Are these chance meetings cosmically designed to bring us together for some unknown reason or cause? Obviously something was happening. In this case, one good turn deserved another. If we are all energy, then on some psychic level, we are transmitting certain vibrations that polarize specific energy into our electromagnetic field. These connections are examples of the merging of realities that cannot be measured by the physical laws of time and space of a three-dimensional world.

One must remember that all circumstances grow out of thought. The outer world of circumstance is shaped by the inner world of thought. Synchronicity or coincidence is really divine intelligence acting upon our thoughts. I have heard hundreds of stories from people about how things just happen to fall into place without any effort. "If I had tried, I couldn't have made this happen," is often the comment. This is exactly the case in the following episode.

I'LL VOUCH FOR HIM

At the early stages of my work as a clairvoyant, I needed a reliable car and didn't have a lot of cash. In Los Angeles a car was a necessity. After several weeks of looking around, it became apparent that my budget didn't accommodate the kind of car I needed.

One evening a friend invited me to an outdoor musical production. As I was waiting for the show to start, I felt a tap on my shoulder. Turning around, I was greeted by another friend seated in the row behind me. "I heard you were looking for a car," he remarked. "Did you find one?"

"No," I said. "What I can afford won't last very long in this city."

He asked me, "Would you settle for a Mercedes?" He was the general manager of the local dealership and had a used one in mint condition.

I agreed to go and see it the next morning.

It was a dream car. But financing was going to be a problem.

At the bank, the financial officer looked at me sympathetically and said, "If you can put down another two or three thousand dollars, we can work it out." The other option was to pay a lot more than I could afford in monthly payments. The bank did not finance used cars beyond a three-year loan, and I needed five years. Since the loan officer knew I was a friend of the boss, she made an extra effort to help me out. "I'll call the bank manager and see if there is anything else we can do for you."

As she began to talk to him on the phone, the conversation was interrupted on the other end of the line.

After a pause, she stammered, "Oh, yes, sir. How nice to talk to you. . . . I'm fine. . . . Oh, it's about a used-car loan for a customer. He's a young man who needs a five-year loan. . . . His name? James Van Praagh. . . . Excuse me? . . . Oh, well, thank you very much, sir. Have a wonderful day yourself!"

"Who *are* you?" asked the loan officer as she got off the phone. She explained that while she was talking to the bank manager, the bank president walked into his office and snatched the phone away from him. "He wanted to know what I was calling about. That's when he asked for your name. He told me to give you anything you needed. He said, 'I'll vouch for him.' "

I was stunned.

"Are you a friend of his?" she asked.

"No," I replied. "I don't think so."

Needless to say, I got my car.

I was amazed and curious about this bank president. How did he know me? Eventually I discovered that a year earlier, a friend of a friend of his had called a friend of a friend of mine seeking help. I was finally tracked down and did a reading for his wife. She was desperately depressed after the death of her daughter. After her reading, she showed me a suicide note that she had written. Her contact with spirit and her daughter gave her enough hope not to end it all.

In my wildest imagination, I could not have planned this scenario. A person whom I never met was able to help me when I needed it because I had helped someone else. It was a beautiful miracle, and I thanked the universe for giving it to me.

BIG AL

I always feel honored to witness the wonderment and joy of miracles or, as I call them, blessings from spirit. The following anecdote demonstrates not only how a spirit's perception changes when it passes into the light, but also how we on earth don't always understand the message, or the importance of it, until much later.

David came to me to contact his mother, who had passed over several years before. He said that she had been instrumental in shaping his life, and he wanted to know if she was still keeping an eye on him.

Sometimes when I open myself to the spirit world for someone, the person he seeks does not come through. In most instances the spirit with the strongest desire to give a message is the one that communicates. Such was the case with David.

"There is a spirit insistent on coming through, but it is not your mother. He tells me that you knew one another for many years. He shows himself to me as being bald with gray hair on the sides. He wears a beautifully tailored dark suit," I told David.

"Do you know his name?" David asked.

"Well, if he impresses me with a name, I will relay it to you. In the meantime, he is lighting up a cigar and blowing the smoke right at me."

This did not ring a bell for David. I kept sending

mental messages to the spirit to give me more specific information. "He is showing me Las Vegas. He is giving me the name of Betsy. Now he is smiling. He is saying that he did not always do nice things, and he has been busy trying to right some of the wrongs he did in life. He speaks of someone named Jill. Does any of this information ring true for you?"

"Yeah. Jill is my wife. Is he related to her?"

I could tell David was hard at work trying to decipher the messages.

"This man is showing me a cannon on wheels. Strange. It looks like it is made out of gold. Does this make sense?"

"No, I don't understand it, James. Are you sure this person came for me? I don't have a relative like that. I don't understand the cannon. Sorry. Is there someone else around?"

I was beginning to get frustrated, but knew from experience that this is sometimes how spirit works, and that what I was hearing was real. I knew that David was not recalling this particular person at this particular moment, but that this man was significant. So much so that I could not feel anyone else's energy around him. It seemed that the bald-headed man was determined to take center stage. I could only listen and transmit the message.

"He is giving me the name of Steven and is pointing to a Corvette," I said.

David shook his head no. I continued anyway. "Well, please keep all this information. One day you may completely understand it. This bald-headed man is saying that you are not sleeping because you bring your work home with you. Now he is showing me a zipper, or he is trying to zip something up. It looks like the zipper is broken. I don't understand this. Do you?"

"Well, today I put on a pair of slacks and the zipper didn't work. Could that be it?"

"Yes, it could be, but I don't know. He is talking about the zipper not working. Do you know the name of Dorman?" I asked.

Finally, a piece of information David recognized. His face lit up like a Christmas tree. "Yes, that's my boss, Paul Dorman. Maybe this guy is a relative of his."

"Yes, he might know him. He does now, he says, laughing. He has a hearty laugh. I must tell you that this man says he wasn't honest with you, and he is apologizing for that. He is telling me that he never knew you were such a decent person. He feels guilty about something he did to you," I told him.

"I don't understand."

I decided to stop and take a rest. After a few minutes I began again to see if I would be able to get anything else. I was given the impression of a bicycle with stingray handlebars. The bike was very popular in the 1960s. Then I saw the letter A.

"He is still here and now showing me a big A. Do you understand it."

"I will have to think about it, James. Sorry."

"One more thing. This man is telling me he has been helping you and has put you in a place he always promised you would be. He is giving me the name of Wesley."

After a few moments David said, "Yes, I used to work with a Wesley. But that was a long time ago."

I then related how this bald-headed man was holding the gold cannon on a key chain. "He is apologizing to you again. He is saying that he saw how ugly he had been on earth and is attempting to clean up his act. He wants to make things better for you."

Still David did not fully understand who this person was or why he came through.

I turned off the recorder I had used to tape the session and gave the tape to David. "Listen to it after a few weeks, and perhaps something will come to mind."

I knew that David was very disappointed that his mother never showed up.

"I'm sorry. Maybe she will come another time. This man, whoever he is, needed to make amends to you for something."

About a month and a half later, I walked into my office after returning from a lecture tour back east. I listened to the messages on the phone machine and heard David's voice. He sounded nearly hysterical. "I need to see you right away," was the message. I called him back and arranged to have dinner with him that evening.

When I walked into the restaurant, David was waiting for me. "Thank you for coming to see me, James." He began to talk nonstop for the next hour. "I went back home after our reading and told my wife, Jill, that nothing happened. I threw the tape into a kitchen drawer. A week later Jill was waiting for me when I came home from work. She had listened to the tape and told me who the bald-headed man was. I couldn't believe it. I was so stupid. I should have known. Please forgive me," David pleaded.

"That's all right. Please don't worry about it. It is part of the communication process. It isn't always as clear and precise as we would hope it to be."

"James, everything you said made sense. When I first moved to California back in the sixties, I got a job with a bald-headed, short man whom we called Big Al. That's what the A meant."

I smiled at him. He was obviously very excited.

"Big Al was a bastard. I took care of him, and he promised that he would take care of me in return. I lied for him and covered up for him when his wife called. Al met a woman at a convention in Vegas. Her name was Betsy. He had an affair with her for two years. One Christmas he was so busy with Betsy that he forgot to get his daughter a Christmas present. I went out and bought her a bicycle. Just like you said, with stingray handlebars! I said it was from her father."

"Amazing." I responded.

"And the zipper! How could I not understand the zipper? I worked in the garment industry. We used to have a slogan that our zippers never got stuck. Once my wife mentioned Big Al, everything you said made sense. I guess I didn't want to remember. Even the name of Wesley and the Corvette. Wesley was a big client from Chicago, and Al wanted to impress him. He knew Wesley had a thing for Corvettes, so I arranged to get him a pristine, fully loaded Corvette as a gift from the company. We got his account, and Big Al got all the praise."

I sat there taking it all in.

"I worked for Al for fifteen years. He promised me a promotion to the top office on the top floor with windows on every side. That's what he promised me for all of my hard work, but he lied. He promoted a new guy named Steven into that position. When I went into his office and complained, he just sat behind his desk, puffing on his cigar. He said, 'I guess ya have ta work faster and harder next time.' I was so pissed off, I quit."

"That's an incredible story, David. Thank you for sharing it with me. I am so happy that everything fell into place for you."

"Wait. There's more. Now it gets weird."

"What?" I asked.

"Last month I was given a promotion by my boss, Paul Dorman. He took me to my new office on the top floor of the building. It had a panoramic view of the city, something I always wanted. When I was looking in my desk to see if I could find the keys to the filing cabinets, I found two keys on a brass key ring in the shape of a cannon with two wheels."

"Wow," I said in amazement.

"I'm not finished. A couple of days ago, I met with my boss to go over some new accounts. That was when I asked him why he hired me. Paul told me that he was really impressed with my background and experience. He had called all my former employers except for the garment manufacturer I had worked for years ago because they had gone out of business. He said it was between another guy and me until he got a call from a former employer who said that I was the best in the business. I asked him the name of this guy, and he said he couldn't forget it. He called himself Big Al."

At this point David's face grew pale. He stared at me with saucer eyes. "James, Big Al has been dead for five years!"

Spirit does work in mysterious ways, but nothing really surprises me anymore. I find that spirits are involved in our everyday affairs and help us to grow in ways that we may not even know. They also watch out for us and keep us from danger and destructive influences. The most important message I have learned as a medium is that first and foremost, we are all spirit. Whether we are here on earth in physical bodies or whizzing from place to place at the speed of a thought in the spiritual realms, we are all connected.

Spirit may provide the miracles of life, but we have to be in the space in which to receive them. It takes faith to open the door to divine intervention and courage to give up control, separation, and isolation. We always have the freedom to choose how we wish to respond to whatever life presents to us. With a forgiving heart, it certainly is possible to let go and let God.

chapter 8

SPIRITUAL CHOICES

Solving Everyday Problems
Through Psychic Ability

I have demonstrated in the preceding chapters that we all have the ability to tap into our inner resources. We can seek the support of our spirit guides, angels, and loved ones on the other side. It is only natural now that you will want to use your psychic awareness on a regular basis to help solve everyday problems. Sometimes one method will work better than another. With enough practice and confidence, you will find the way that works best for you. No matter the obstacle, I know that the right use of your psychic ability will bring you closer to resolving any solution. It is my sincere desire that you will be able to make ordinary decisions from an extrasensory approach. I call these spiritual choices.

What is a spiritual choice? When we make choices from a spiritual perspective, we approach a problem from a holistic point of view. We take into account the physical, emotional, psychological, and, most important, the invisible or spiritual consequences. A spiritual choice is not one driven by our ego, which is a choice made out of fear. A spiritual choice is one by which we don't accrue more karmic debt in this lifetime, only to have to neutralize it in another.

Making the right decisions can sometimes be a painful process. When we look to the outside world for answers, we inevitably stumble along feeling confused and apprehensive. For instance, your neighbor buys a new car, and you think that if he can afford one, so can you. After buying one, you find that you have overextended yourself financially, putting more pressure on yourself and your family. Another example: You decide to take a job that really is not for you. The money is good, so you convince yourself that you will learn to like it. Unfortunately, you have created unneeded stress from a job that leaves you unfulfilled. Yet another: You get married because of some external pressure—your parents want grandchildren, your friends are already married. Surprise, surprise: You find that you spend many hours arguing with your partner because you made a decision for all the wrong reasons. In these choices, the decision hurts you, and it hurts others. You must undo what you have done. Reparations often come at an inconvenient time and place. There is no such thing as a shortcut.

On the other hand, a spiritual choice is a mindful choice and takes into account how the consequences may affect others. This does not mean that spiritual choices are made to please other people. A spiritual choice is not cause for sacrificing your needs because you feel another person's needs are more justified. When you are a martyr, you feel resentful. In the end, everyone suffers to some extent when you let your ego make decisions.

My belief is that when you do what's right for you, harming no one, you are being true. Other people may not like it, but that may be the reason you are around— to teach others to be more flexible, or to set an example of how to be true to yourself. Chances are, if you're lying to yourself, you're lying to others. If you're true to yourself, you're true to the world.

So much in life seems to be a struggle; it makes us wonder why we are here. If there really is a God, why doesn't God do a better job at helping us? Why do we get diseases? Why are our children shot in school? Why do the bad guys get all the attention? I believe that the most difficult challenges in life are really blessings in disguise. They afford us opportunities to go deep within ourselves and discover our own light. Instead of asking helpless, rhetorical questions, making a spiritual choice takes the struggle out of a situation, helps us accept it for what it is, and teaches us the way to a solution.

I FOUND GOD

A few years ago I attended a benefit for the environmental organization Greenpeace. I know it sounds a bit fantastic, but I am basically a very shy person. Being shy, I spent the better part of the evening off to the side observing others mingling on the floor. Occasionally I would wander into the crowd to seek out a morsel of food. In one instance, as my hand reached for a spinach pastry, another hand had the same idea. I looked up and saw a familiar face.

"Marky!" I said in surprise.

Mark looked a little wiser and more mature since I had seen him eight years earlier. In fact, I was shocked to see him at such an event. He never struck me as someone who would be overly concerned with the environment.

I originally met Mark as a client. He had come to me on the advice of a counselor who hoped that he might be able to resolve past conflicts with his mother if he had the opportunity to contact her in spirit. The reading was successful in that Mark's mother did come through. However, at the time, Mark was still unable to forgive her.

Mark had had a difficult childhood. His brother was killed in cold blood right before his eyes. His father was an alcoholic and his mother a severe drug abuser. He was shuffled from one foster home to another and never had a true sense of what it meant to be part of a family. By the time he reached ninth grade, he could no longer take the bullying and sarcastic comments from the insensitive kids at school, so he dropped out. He moved into his aunt and uncle's home, where he was sexually abused. Mark ran away from that environment and was able to share a small apartment with a friend. The last time I saw him, he was working in a video store.

That evening, with spinach pastries on our plates, we proceeded to an outdoor porch so we could catch up. Now that I think of it, I remember saying to myself, Someday I hope I get a chance to share his story with the rest of the world.

Mark began, "I quit the video store, you know. They accused me of stealing money from the night deposits, which I hadn't. After I lost my job, I had no money, so I couldn't pay the rent. That was the beginning of my descent into hell."

Like his mother, Mark entered the world of drugs. "I was so hooked on crack that I am basically amazed that I am here to talk to you tonight."

"How did you get out of it?" I asked.

Mark looked at his plate, then turned to me and said, "Actually, I found God——"

I thought, Uh-oh, he's going to start preaching.

Mark interrupted my thoughts. "Inside of me," he finished.

I didn't quite understand where he was coming from until he explained further. "I was literally lying on the curb staring at a billboard of Tom Hanks in some movie. I remember thinking, This guy is nobody special, just a guy on television who made a movie. What's so different between him and me? I can do that! I can have everyone look up to me and know who I am too. As soon as those thoughts crossed my mind, a car backed over my foot. A woman got out. She looked at me and got very upset. I was so out of it, but somehow she managed to get me to the hospital."

"That was nice of her," I observed.

"She was really an angel sent by God. When I was in the hospital, I went through detox. That's when I did a lot of soul searching. I had to get out of my own way, so to speak, and let God, or whatever power, do the work. I realized that there was no one to blame but me if my life got screwed up. I had to take responsibility for the future, and I knew I needed some support to make things change. That is what living is all about."

I could not believe that this was the same guy I had met eight years ago.

"It was that woman who ran over me. She helped me to believe in myself again. She wanted to help me. I mattered to her. She said she could see the light in my eyes. She introduced me to a friend who owned a glass company, a guy named Roger. I began to work for Roger and eventually had this idea about etching color designs onto the glass. That was the beginning. Roger let me create my own pieces and sell them. My designs are now all over the world."

"That's incredible." I said. "Whatever happened to that lady?"

"There she is over there," Mark said as he pointed to a pregnant woman. She was a Gwyneth Paltrow look-alike.

I turned to Mark and said, "She's pregnant."

"Yes, we are expecting our first baby in June. We know it's a girl, and we are debating whether to call her Angeline or Violet."

I was smiling. His story sent warmth to my soul. This was indeed a celebration. One life about to be born while another life was given a second chance.

"Congratulations," I said as Mark introduced me to his kindhearted wife.

Here was a young man who had faced many obstacles in life. But with awareness, inner strength, determination, and self-assuredness, he was able to accomplish more than anyone would have expected. His journey is nothing less than a miracle and a testament to the power of choice. Today when I see Mark's beautiful glass bowls and plates in stores, I can't help thinking that life is good.

RESPONSIBILITY

Most of the time, people passively let life happen to them instead of taking charge and choosing to live it for themselves. Like Mark, we all have free choice. He could have stayed in the gutter, but he chose to get out of it. People forget that the choice is always theirs—even in the most difficult of circumstances.

With choice comes responsibility. For many, responsibility is a challenging subject. In so many ways, it is easier to indulge ourselves in the attitude that the world has dealt us an impossible situation, and we deserve pity for it. Instead of taking responsibility and possibly blame, we point to others and say it's their fault. Parents, teachers, and society are easily classified as the culprits in a consciousness that doesn't take responsibility. Victim consciousness is the product of ego, not spirit. If we don't take responsibility for our actions and ourselves, no one can expect too much of us.

On the other hand, there are people who suffer from misguided feelings of responsibility, who believe that they are responsible for everyone else's life working out. By focusing so much on others, they refrain from being responsible for their own lives. Women, historically, have been conditioned to become the victims of other people's needs. *How can I do what I want when I have an aging mother to take care of, and small children to raise?* It's difficult to break the programs and conditions with which we were raised, but it's possible. I have been fortunate to witness the miracles of such a liberation over and over again.

Victim consciousness is a fear-based consciousness that disempowers us. We lose control over our lives. Blaming others for our misfortune is a way of saying, "I am not in charge here. You are." We can only be victims if we allow it. The willingness to be self-responsible is a big step in attaining a spiritually balanced life.

Even if it appears unbelievable and unreasonable, nothing ever happens to us without our permission. How can that be? I am often told by people, "I didn't give permission to get cancer." But we do on some level of consciousness. In making this observation, I do not want you to feel guilty for a life-threatening illness.

Remember, soul evolution is the reason that we are here. Your illness, or loss, or predicament is a part of your soul's growth. You are made up of the sum total of past incarnations. The willingness to heal and learn, and tasks to be completed in each lifetime are in your makeup. Karmic decisions and obligations are part of the process. If it's in your karmic contract to complete

a relationship in this lifetime that was left uncompleted
in a previous life, you can't get around it if you try.

Illness, the loss of a loved one, and misfortune might
be ways to learn humility, surrender, and faith. Your illness may be a way to help other people learn to love
more. Your predicament may teach you how to stand
up for your rights. Your loss may help other people
from having to experience the same kind of tragedy.
We are multidimensional beings of light. The purpose
of our existence goes beyond physical outcomes.
Ultimately, we have all come here to learn to love—not
romantically, but unconditionally. A gift of love can be
painfully disguised.

Often the most difficult choice to make is the one
that might hurt someone. Leaving an unfulfilled relationship, firing an employee who is not doing his or
her share of the work, and telling a friend an unpleasant
truth are choices that might cause immediate discomfort. However, in the long run, such a choice may turn
out to have a great liberating force. Your decision might
catapult another into reexamining her life or help
someone to understand his patterns of dysfunction.
Your choice to leave may provide a person with a true
incentive to heal. Many times it takes great pain to set a
life-transforming process into motion.

MY GRANDMOTHER'S GUIDANCE

As you are well aware by now, I am constantly in contact with my spirit guides because of the work I do. I

have learned to trust in their guidance and their support. This is true for anyone.

A young man by the name of Tony came to see me
for a reading. We had a chance to talk after his session
was over. He said that he was vacillating on an important decision. "I was offered a job with a new employer.
If I accept the offer, I will have to relocate and go back
to the East Coast. I am not sure that it's the best thing
for me. I asked some of my friends, and they have urged
me to stay where I am. I think they believe I will be
lonely without them or my family. And they could be
right."

"How do you feel?" I asked.

"I'm not sure. I think it's a great opportunity profes-
sionally and financially."

"It's difficult to be torn between your mind and
emotions," I commented.

"Yeah, it's confusing all right. I just don't want to
make a mistake. I thought I would get the answers from
this reading."

"Perhaps you already have."

"What do you mean?" Tony said with a puzzled look
on his face.

"You have tapped into the spirit world. You know that
there is more than just the physical existence. Trust in
spirit and let your mind and emotions sit this one out."

I gave him his tape and told him to go home and
meditate. "Go within and talk to your spirit loved ones.
Ask them to guide you in your decision. Let me know
what happens."

A week later Tony called to give me a report. "I sat in

my bedroom, lit a candle, and prayed. I asked for help in making the right decision, like you told me. After a while I felt warmth inside my body and a complete calmness. I could hear my grandmother's voice. At first I thought I was making it up inside my head. Then I heard her say what she used to repeat to me all the time. 'Turn off that TV and go outside in the fresh air.' I figured that she was telling me to stop listening to others and to take the job. I would be living in a place that would force me to be outdoors more in nature . . . in fresh air."

"Sounds like you're moving, then," I replied.

"Well, here's the clincher. When I walked out of my bedroom, the TV was on in the den. As I went to shut it off, there on the screen was a picture of the city I would be moving to. I felt it was a confirmation that I had made the right decision."

We can ask our guardian angels, the archangels, our spirit guides, and our ancestors to give us help. There are many ways they can give us signals. Our job is to quiet our minds and our egos, open our hearts, and listen.

A LEAP OF FAITH

Eileen is a friend of mine, and several years ago she had the opportunity to open her own business. As she said, "It was my life's dream to be my own boss." Being a go-getter, Eileen was anxious to get started. She began looking at office space and found something that she thought would be perfect. She made an appointment with the real estate agent to negotiate the terms of the lease.

She told me, "I was so happy and confident that I was taking the next step to opening my business."

However, as the day of the meeting drew near, Eileen began to feel uneasy. "I had second thoughts that the space might be too expensive. I had a strong impulse to postpone the meeting until a later date, but I was also afraid that I would lose the perfect location," she declared.

"What did you do?" I asked.

"I couldn't think of one reason for postponing the date, other than I felt nervous. But I decided that I didn't want to face the landlord and act like an anxious lamebrain in front of him. I had to go into that meeting with the persuasion and conviction that I was the businesswoman I said I was."

Trusting in her intuition, Eileen postponed the meeting to negotiate the lease. "The fear of losing that space was so overwhelming I had this internal argument going on inside my head."

"What happened?" I inquired.

"Three days later the real estate agent called, and said that the landlord had come down in price because he wanted to rent the space to me and was afraid I was looking elsewhere for a better deal."

Eileen was exhilarated and rented the office. She learned to pay attention to her intuitive feelings. By choosing not to keep her appointment, she was able to negotiate better terms. It was exactly what she needed to do to relieve some of the pressure of starting a new business.

When you believe in yourself, like my friend Eileen, you have faith and trust in your connectedness to truth. The energy needed to materialize your desire cannot flow freely if you are fearful about the outcome. There is no room for fear in spiritual decision making. Ultimately you must trust that there is no wrong decision. Any decision leads to your growth and reaching new levels of consciousness. It might be a challenging process, but it gets easier with practice.

THE TREASURES WITHIN

When we find ourselves in horrific situations, we wonder how we can muster the courage to get out of our own way so that the divine within us can take over. The following reading exemplifies the enormous difficulties one woman had to overcome before realizing her true potential.

I was in Chicago lecturing to a crowd of six hundred people. A spirit calling himself Hal impressed me with his thoughts. He was a sweet man. I felt as though I were speaking to a professor, and found out later that indeed I had been.

Hal impressed me to go to a woman standing against a wall in the back of the room. I wasn't sure if this woman was part of the hotel staff or one of the guests. This spirit definitely wanted to make a connection with her.

I pointed to the woman and said, "I want to come to you. There is a man here with the name of Hal. He wants to be known to you."

"Yes, I understand. Hal was my best friend."

"I don't know why he is showing me this, but I am seeing Hansel and Gretel. Do you know what this means?" I asked.

"Well . . . my name is Greta," she replied.

"He sounds very much like a teacher. He wants to make sure everything he says is understood precisely."

Greta announced that her friend was once an art professor at Northwestern University. "He was always very articulate when he spoke," she added.

"Greta, this man is telling me about a Richie or Richard and says you don't owe him anything anymore."

Greta looked down and remained silent. Obviously, I had hit a nerve. She did not want to discuss it, but Hal certainly did.

"He says that he has tried to warn you about this Richie person. He is also speaking to me about Saint Luke. Do you understand this?" I asked.

The woman just nodded her head and did not seem to want to say more.

Sometimes, in such a public arena, I find that it is better to see the person privately during the break or at the end of the appearance in order to help. So I thanked Greta, and at the break I asked an assistant to find her in the back of the room and bring her to me so that we could speak further.

Greta came backstage, and we arranged a private

appointment so that we could continue the important message from Hal. One of my guides informed me that this meeting was going to be very difficult but necessary.

Two days later Greta sat in front of me in my hotel room. We closed our eyes, and I said my opening prayer.

Almost immediately I picked up several spirits around her. "There is a man standing to your left. He is a father figure, rather tall, and is smoking a cigarette. He has trouble speaking before he dies and points to his throat. Did his passing have something to do with the throat?"

"Yes. He died of throat cancer," Greta said.

"He comes with a woman on his side. This would be his mother. She is giving me the name of Nell and is showing me a cornfield and a farm."

"Yes, that's right. My grandmother lived on a farm in Iowa. I didn't know her," Greta added.

"That's fine. She just wants to be acknowledged and let you know that she is with your father. There is also a woman here on your right side. This is strange. She says she doesn't want to scare you. I feel as though she has a Ca or Ke in her name. She is very slow. I can tell that she does not really want to be here because her energy is very faint. She is connected to your father through marriage, because I am shown a ring," I told her.

I could see that this was not a subject that Greta wanted to discuss, but it was necessary.

"Yes, that is my mother. I understand. Go on."

"This lady was very ill before she passed over. Did she have a nurse?"

Greta looked down toward the floor as if embarrassed. She hesitated but finally answered. "I . . . ah . . . I took care of her. At least, I tried to. She was difficult. She weighed a lot, and it was hard work. I didn't mean . . ." Greta became overwhelmed and faltered. "I didn't mean for her to be alone. I just went to the store for a few things." She began to cry.

"Did you mother have trouble walking?" I asked.

"Yes. She couldn't walk. I had to help her out of bed. She wasn't steady on her feet."

"Your mother is all right now. She said that her dying was not your fault and that you must put all that behind you. Don't blame yourself. It isn't right. She will help you as you have helped her."

Greta was crying so hard, I had to stop the reading for a few moments until she calmed down.

The spirit who had come through at the public demonstration then joined us.

"I have Hal here again. He tells me that he took you to art museums in New York."

"Yes, he did. I love you, Hal. Thank you," Greta said happily.

Hal continued to talk about their friendship and all the experiences they shared together.

Greta looked at me and asked, "May I ask Hal a question, please?"

"Of course. Go ahead," I replied.

Greta looked above my head and practically screamed out, "Help me, Hal! Please, help me. I don't know what to do. I can't take it anymore!"

I was completely taken by surprise. I didn't expect

her to react so vehemently. I sat still for a few minutes attempting to hear Hal's reply. I was mystified at his response.

"He is saying, *move.* He wants you to move. He says that he has told you that before. You never listen to him, and he doubts you will listen to him now."

I could see the torment on Greta's face. I wished I could help her to sort herself out, but this was something she obviously had to do on her own. Hal kept telling her to move, and that was all that he said for the rest of the session.

I felt very sad for Greta. I knew that she must be searching for an answer, and like most people, she had expected spirit to wave a magic wand over her, and all of her problems would cease to exist. Well, that doesn't happen. Besides, it would be detrimental to her spiritual growth for her *not* to take responsibility for the choices she made in her life.

More than once, Hal referred to Saint Luke, which he had also mentioned at the public demonstration days earlier.

Greta acknowledged the reference.

I knew this session was difficult for her, but at the same time I knew that it was probably a significant turning point in her life. I continued with the reading.

"Your father is saying to get away from Rich. You must have peace."

"It isn't easy. I don't know what to do. I feel trapped! Can Daddy help me?"

"Your father is saying that you have to do it for yourself. He will help you if you help yourself."

Greta contemplated these words.

"He is talking about your five-year-old birthday and something about a merry-go-round."

"I don't understand."

"He is showing me a box of photographs in a drawer in the bedroom. Look for it. There is a photo with a merry-go-round. When you see this photo, you will understand."

"I can't remember the photo," responded Greta.

After the reading was over, I told Greta to listen to the tape in a few days.

"Perhaps certain things will make more sense." I told her to look for the photograph that her father mentioned.

She agreed. "I'll let you know what happens."

A week came and went, but I didn't hear from Greta. Actually, I didn't hear from her until three years later.

I was in my office going through the mail, and a letter fell to the floor. I picked it up and opened it. It was from Greta. The letter read:

Dear Mr. Van Praagh,

I met you three years ago at a workshop in Chicago. You had brought through my friend Hal, and later you met with me privately for a session. I wanted to write to thank you so much for helping me to change my life. You brought through my family, and they have helped me to see who I am.

Just recently I found the tape of our meeting

and played it again. I am amazed at how much of the information makes sense now. I am so sorry at the time that I wasn't able to say anything. I was too embarrassed. That is why I felt I needed to write this letter.

First of all, I had been married for over fifteen years to an alcoholic and a drug user. He was violent and would hit me. I learned to accept his treatment because I thought he would kill me if I tried to leave. I didn't think enough of myself to do anything.

If you remember, Hal, my best friend, mentioned St. Luke's Hospital several times. He would come to the emergency room after one of Richard's brawls and take me home. He certainly was my hero, but I never listened to him when he begged me to leave Rich.

On the tape my mother, Keri, said that it wasn't my fault that she died. Well, Mr. Van Praagh, for years I blamed myself for her death. The one day that I went to the store and left her alone, she fell off the bed, hit her head, and died. I thought if I had been there, it would not have happened.

Anyway, a year after seeing you, I had a beautiful dream in which my mother, father, and Hal were present. I was a small child, and they were singing "Happy Birthday" to me. I remember everyone telling me to make a wish and blow out the candles. My wish was to be a nurse and help people.

The dream seemed so real. It made me realize that I was not living the life I wanted. While my husband was at work, I packed up my things and left him to stay with my friend. The last thing I packed was the box of pictures you had mentioned in the reading. When I dumped them in a bag, one of the pictures fell out. I looked at it and was dumbfounded. It was a picture of me on my fifth birthday. I was wearing the present my parents gave me. I am enclosing it so that you can see for yourself.

I have been divorced for over a year now. I am living in my own one-bedroom apartment and am completing my nursing course next week. Finally, after thirty-five years, I feel that I have found my true calling and feel free to be myself. I don't know what to say to you. "Thank you" does not seem enough for giving me back my life. I guess it was always there, but I sure had a hard time finding it.

Love,
Greta Straub

P.S. My ex-husband started to go to AA. He has been clean and sober for the past eight months.

Accompanying the letter was a photograph of a little girl in a nurse's costume standing in front of a merry-go-round.

What a wonderful example of a difficult choice that is both empowering and encouraging. It reminds us to stop living for others' expectations of our lives, and to follow our own truths.

DO IT FOR LOVE

When we make decisions driven by our egos, they usually lead us down the wrong path. In this society, especially, we are filled with images of successful, talented, and rich people. We see only the outer circumstances of someone's life and think, I want to be that too. It's okay when other people's successes motivate us. However, we must know that when we act, it must be for love and not for ego's sake.

That was precisely the predicament in which one client had found himself when he came for a reading. Peter showed up at my door dressed in a brilliant blue shirt and black tailored slacks. He looked as if he had stepped out of GQ.

I asked him, "Are you a model?"

"No," he said, smiling, "but people always mistake me for one."

I got started on the reading. "I see a woman with long, dark hair standing behind you. She has a stick in her hand. She is hitting the stick against the palm of her other hand. Does this make sense to you?"

"Definitely," said Peter.

"She is showing me a room with mirrors. It looks like a hall in a theater. Now I see little children lined up next to a bar. It is a room where children are learning dance lessons."

"Yes, she is my old dance teacher from childhood."

"Are you a dancer?" I asked.

"Yes."

"This woman is giving me the letters PIA. Do you understand?"

"Her name is Sophia."

"She is giving me a picture of a young man dancing and dancing. This man is going from one place to another."

"Yes. I have been going on many auditions. I have a goal to be a famous ballet dancer."

"This spirit is now shaking the stick very wildly. She is talking like a strict teacher. You must forget the money and the fame, she is saying adamantly."

I turned my head to the side. The spirit was practically screaming in my ear. I told her to speak more quietly.

The reading went on for another half hour. This spirit scolded Peter for most of the time. I had difficulty maintaining that type of energy.

When we ended the reading, I asked him, "Why was she so upset with you?"

"I guess she is not happy with my performance, and I can't blame her," he said. "I have been so wrapped up in becoming a famous dancer that I started to spend more time schmoozing with the right people and less time practicing."

"Perhaps you want to rethink your decision about being a famous dancer. Maybe you need to focus on being the best dancer you can be," I advised.

"Lately I have been lousy in my auditions and keep getting rejected. Sophia was a stickler for form. My form is a mess. I am too tense, and it shows. I miss the joy and happiness I used to feel when I performed."

"Fame is not a good motivator," I asserted. "It actually inhibits success."

He looked helpless and frustrated. "I don't know if I can get back the passion I once had."

"Start living in the moment," I advised him. "I am sure Sophia will be there to guide you. She thinks you have the talent. Enjoy your dancing. I think you have become too obsessed with your goal. When you change your motive, your energy will change, and your love of dancing will return."

When we have a desire or goal like Peter, we should not focus expressly on it and on some fear that we won't achieve it. When we do so, we are trying to control the outcome of a situation, and we are not giving spirit a chance to get involved. The energy needed to bring forth our desires cannot flow freely if we are obsessing over the material results. Always ask for something with the highest good in mind; then let go and let God.

LET YOUR LIGHT SHINE

In order to make good decisions, first you must know yourself. Most people with whom I have dealt have a rather limited view of themselves. They find it so much easier to criticize themselves instead of respect who they are. We very often feel as though we are alone in life—and to some extent we are, at least in a physical sense. Emotions can blind us and thoughts can confuse us. If we get caught up in our personal losses, fill ourselves with worries and fears, there is no room for light to enter. If we are narrow-minded and eager to criticize, there is no room for the light to penetrate. Using your psychic awareness can help you to make choices based on an internal process, not on external criticisms.

Remember also that choice is a two-way street. We must allow other people the right to make their choices even if we don't agree with them. When you honor another person's decision, by not judging or condemning his behavior, you are coming from a place of unconditional love. Acceptance makes it okay for others to be themselves, to follow their truths. We never know what is important for another person's spiritual growth.

One of the ways you can ask for help is to ask for a sign. Signs from spirit are all around us, and everything speaks to us if we stay aware. I will often say to my spirit guides, "Give me a sign that this is the best decision or that I am on the right track." If I meet with constant resistance, obstacles, and delays about a certain project or decision, I take it as a sign from spirit that I am heading in the wrong direction. My friend Dorothea, who is a gifted psychic, often says, "Sometimes the greatest gift is not getting what we want."

Another way to make healthy decisions is to contemplate the outcome of each possibility. As you visualize different scenarios, be aware of your feelings. Joy is a great way of knowing that you have made the right decision.

When we act with compassion, peace, and dignity in all that we do, we are expressing an illuminated spirit. Spirit is constantly seeking expression through our activities, thoughts, and contributions. It inspires us to work at our greatest level of competence, individuality, and dedication. Seek to express its strength, skill, goodwill, and courage in all that you do so, and spirit's light will shine through you.

chapter 9

TECHNIQUES FOR DEVELOPMENT

*Preparing to Make
the Psychic Connection*

Typically, all of us live our lives through past experiences, criticisms, and judgments. All too often, this hampers our soul's development. By training our mind and living in the present, we allow new opportunities to enter our lives. The techniques in this chapter will prove more successful if you do them with an objective viewpoint and an open mind. You will begin to see life very differently—bear that in mind as you begin each of the following exercises, which can be done alone or with partners.

Depending on your level of interest, you can practice these exercises as often as you like. You may want to cleanse your aura on a daily basis, while doing other exercises once or twice a week. Others, like defining and clearing a space, can be done as the need arises. Automatic writing and dream recall must be done regularly if you want to achieve beneficial results. Joining a development circle is a step toward more serious study. Ultimately any and all of these practices are necessary if you want to develop your psychic awareness in earnest.

PRELIMINARY GROUNDWORK

Anything you attempt, whether it is fixing something in the house, painting a picture, or taking a trip, requires preparation. The same is true for techniques in intuitive development. It is important, therefore, that you prepare properly. Take at least five to ten minutes for the following *preliminary groundwork* before you begin these exercises, otherwise your results will be inconsequential.

Sit in a comfortable position, making sure your spine is straight. If you slouch, energy cannot move up and down the body easily. Imagine a wire pulling you straight up from the top of your head. Close your eyes and take several deep breaths. As you do, visualize each breath coming into the body like a stream of golden light. This light touches and fills your every cell, organ, and muscle. With each breath you feel invigorated. As you exhale, imagine a gray mist exiting the body. This mist represents any excess energy, anxiety, fear, nervousness, or apprehension that you may have.

Next, imagine that you are sitting in the center of your body. Visualize that you are looking out of your body from behind the middle of your forehead, right behind the brow. This is your third eye center.

Last, visualize three cords. One is tied to the base of

your spine and the other two are connected to each ankle. See these cords going straight down to the center of the earth. Imagine three big rocks at the center of the earth, and tie a cord to each rock. Concentrate on moving any excess energy in your space along the cords into the earth. At the same time, visualize the energy of Mother Earth traveling up the cords healing you and anchoring you to the earth. You are now grounded and centered properly to begin your work. Remember to be patient, confident, and joyful in your approach.

DEVELOPING YOUR FIVE SENSES

The goal of these next exercises is to make you more aware of the world around you. As you hone your five senses, you will strengthen them as well as the corresponding astral senses. Remember to do your *preliminary groundwork* first. Keep a notebook nearby to summarize your insights.

Sight

Most of us take our sight for granted and usually choose to see what we want to see and to ignore what we don't. This exercise will help to expand your vision.

Choose a large flower and place it in a vase on the center of the table. Close your eyes and take several deep breaths. Open your eyes and observe everything about the flower as if you were looking through a magnifying glass. As you look at the flower, try to imagine that you can see through it. See everything you can about this flower. Look at its distinctive shape and color. Is it darker or lighter in some areas than others? Perceive as much as you can and describe what you see; write down the characteristics of the flower.

Once completed, close your eyes once again and take a few deep breaths to bring you back to center. Open your eyes and look at the flower, but this time with a sense of seeing beyond the surface to its personality. Realize that it is a living being. What traits can you see in it? Does it remind you of someone or something? Does it stir emotions inside you?

Again, write everything you sense this second time in your notepad and compare the two lists. You will be surprised at the observations. Finally, don't judge or criticize what you saw or did not see. Enjoy the experience.

Hearing

Arrange on a table several objects of the same substance, such as a wooden spoon and a piece of wood, and a metal spoon and a piece of metal, like tin. This exercise will help you concentrate on discerning the variations between similar but differing sounds.

In order to heighten your awareness of one sense over another, sometimes it is best to close off one or more of your other senses. This is true for hearing. Place a blindfold over your eyes and sit silently for a few seconds. Become accustomed to the sounds in the room.

Next, pick up the wooden spoon and tap it. Now pick up the piece of wood and tap it. Listen carefully to the nuances of each object's sound. Can you notice a difference between them? Now try the same thing with the metal spoon and the other metal item. Go back and forth between the two and become aware of the differences.

When you are finished, keep the blindfold on for another ten minutes and tune into every trivial sound you hear around your house or from the outside. Be aware of the highest tones to the lowest. You can practice this exercise wherever you are simply by closing your eyes and listening. You will be surprised to find how sensitive your hearing will become.

Touch

Place several items with different textures in front of you, such as a sweater, a sponge, and a rock. Once again, place a blindfold over your eyes. You can even use earplugs for this exercise. Again the purpose is to help narrow your focus to a particular sense.

Begin by touching each item with your fingers and hands. What does the surface feel like? Do any thoughts or emotions stir inside of you? How would you describe what you are feeling? How does each item differ? Write your observations on your notepad.

Next, go outside and walk around your garden. If you don't have a garden, go to a park. Find an area with trees and shrubs and flowers. Close your eyes and touch the trees. Attend to your feeling, so that it will be recorded in your memory. The same with the flowers and shrubs. Feel the leaves on the plant. Try to focus only on touch.

While you are outside, open your hands so that your palms face out. Feel the wind going through them. This is a delicate sensation. The more you can detect the subtleties in life, the more skillful you will become at reaching spirit, and the more joy you will experience.

Taste

Although taste is a sense that is underrated in psychic development, it is nevertheless quite important. This exercise is usually everyone's favorite. In order to differentiate between tastes, you may have to rinse your mouth with some water after each flavor.

Try this exercise with a slice of lemon, a piece of chocolate, a cup of stale coffee, and a peppermint. Use a blindfold and earplugs. Begin to taste each item. Notice any emotional reaction. Do you like the taste or not? What about the texture?

I am sure that you have heard the expression, "That leaves a bad taste in my mouth." This figure of speech applies to our intuitive sensibility. It is important to fully be aware of this sense—it is possible to receive psychic impressions through your taste buds.

Smell

We rely on the sense of smell much more than we realize. There are several methods of sensitizing and enhancing your sense of smell. First, gather several items like perfume or aftershave lotion, a fragrant rose, incense, and a variety of fresh herbs such as lavender or rosemary. Use the blindfold and earplugs.

Hold each item to your nose and take in its distinct fragrance. What is your reaction when you inhale the fragrance? Does it remind you of something? Often aromas bring up memories. Do you like the smell or not?

Another technique is to spend a day being conscious of scents. If you can, write the descriptions in your notepad along with the feelings or memories they conjure. You will be surprised and delighted by what you perceive. Very often, our loved ones in spirit exhibit some scent when they first try to contact us.

Another way to develop your sense of smell is through aromatherapy. I use a variety of essential oils or incense for meditation, purification, and protection of my space. Aromatherapy incorporates natural elements of wood, herbs, and flowers, and each scent has a certain frequency or vibration associated with it. Therefore, when used correctly, these aromas can raise your energy levels, assist you in reaching a meditative state, and protect your environment.

Incense has been used for thousands of years by people while praying. American Indians "smudge" their surroundings with bundled sticks of sage to ward off negative vibrations and clear their auras. The rising smoke signifies prayers ascending to the heavens to be heard. Many religious traditions use incense and smoke to purify and sanctify a sacred space before a spiritual ceremony takes place.

ACHIEVING AN ALTERED STATE OF CONSCIOUSNESS

First, perform your *preliminary groundwork*. The next thing you will attempt is to fully relax the body. Tense and relax each muscle group, starting with the toes and slowly working your way up to the head. As you release the tension in the muscles, you will feel the stress dissipating and the body become relaxed.

Next, pay attention to your breathing. With each inhalation, feel more and more relaxed. When you exhale, let go of the demands and concerns of your day. Just relax, just be.

As you continue to breathe, imagine going down a staircase. With each step down, you become more relaxed. As you step, say the word *love* or *joy* or *peace*. Welcome the awareness of that word into your space and into your own self-expression. Notice how you feel as you say this word. Let your mind concentrate on this word. Every time your mind wanders, focus on the word. Be aware of how this word expands your reality. As you continue going down the steps, you become more and more relaxed. When you reach the bottom of the steps, you are now in a sacred and safe space for your explorative work.

FEELING THE ENERGY IN A ROOM

Begin with the *preliminary groundwork*. As you remain centered in your own sacred space, close your eyes and open your hands to feel the energy in the room. You will get some sort of initial impression. It might be emotional or mental or physical. You might even have an auditory sense of the energy.

Walk toward a part of the room to which you feel drawn. As you get closer, analyze the energy you are picking up and describe it. Does it feel dense or light? Can you sense any colors or forms? Does this energy come with a personality? Is there a change in temperature? What are your final observations of this room? You can go through every room in a house and get very different reactions from each.

If you wish to change the energy in a room, go to the center of the room. Close your eyes and visualize a huge golden sun coming into the room. The rays of the sun fill the room with a loving, joyful light. Notice the difference in the energy of the room after you do this visualization.

RELEASING MENTAL AND EMOTIONAL BAGGAGE

We cannot help carrying the mental and emotional energy that we have accumulated through our daily experiences. We absorb energy from our family members, friends, and even strangers. The more sensitive you are, the more susceptible you are to picking up other people's garbage. If you retain this energy in your space, you can become disturbed. Therefore, you must remember to assess your energy on a daily basis and clear out any unnecessary baggage. This is the next step in becoming more spiritually receptive.

After your groundwork exercise, sit in a comfortable position with your spine straight. Close your eyes and begin breathing deeply. With each breath, go deeper into relaxation. Become aware of the energy that surrounds you. Start with the area three to five inches in front of you, behind you, and to either side, then gradually extend this awareness out farther. As you attune yourself to this space, read every part of it. Now notice if you can detect anyone else's energy in your space. Become aware of any emotions that are present. Do they belong to you? Are they someone else's? If these emotions are not yours, surround them with golden light and, in your mind, lovingly send them back to their source. Allow into your space only those images and emotions that nurture you and your spiritual development. Then ask that any energy that you passed to others during the day be returned to you.

DAILY AFFIRMATION

Try to start each day as a celebration of life. Before you get out of bed in the morning, take one moment to thank the great creative force for giving you another day to experience the incredible wonders of life. I always say:

Thank you, dear God, for another day of life.
May it bring to me all the necessary experiences
so that my soul can learn and grow with the protection of the light of love and all that is good.

This affirmation starts your day with a positive focus.

TUNING INTO THE BREATH

As you get deeply involved in intuitive work, your
practice becomes more intense. This exercise will help
you to go deeper within yourself. I suggest that everyone do this technique in my development circles.

All life begins and ends with the breath. It is the
breath that carries the prana, or life-force energy,
through our bodies. The most important thing to
remember is that because the breath sustains life, we
need to understand it, learn how to use it, and respect
it. Use it to open the door to the invisible. Paying
attention to your breath is the first step in learning how
to accomplish this.

Sit in a comfortable position and close your eyes. As
you breathe in and out, observe each breath—don't try
to control or change it. Gradually, with each succeeding
breath, attempt to inhale for a few seconds more and
exhale all the way out. Continue this for a few minutes.
Then breathe naturally. You will soon notice that the
breath will expand and contract in its own timing, very
much like the ebb and flow of the ocean tides. Don't
try to control it. Just let it happen naturally.

MEDITATION FOR MENTAL AND EMOTIONAL HARMONY

To be open to spirit contact, and to reach the highest of spiritual realms, you must be in proper alignment mentally, emotionally, and physically. You must constantly strive to keep your body and mind in harmony. The following is a meditation to assist you in finding balance.

Begin with your *preliminary groundwork*. Now, keeping the rhythm of the breath constant, be aware that with every exhalation the body becomes more and more relaxed.

Focus your attention from the seat of knowing located in the third eye center. Become aware of the energy space above and below you, as well as in front, behind, and to either side of you. Become familiar with your own energy.

In your mind's eye, imagine a large pink rose. See it open slowly, petal by petal. Then use the rose to scan each part of your energy space, starting with your head and shoulder area. As you do so, can you see any images or faces? Do you hear or feel anything? Are these impressions associated with loving, happy, or nurturing thoughts? Or do they promote fear, sadness, or anxiety? If you experience the latter, place the person, situation, or thought in the middle of the rose, and see the rose absorb that energy until the feelings associated with it are gone.

Repeat this process throughout your entire energy space. Notice that the more you fill the rose, the larger it becomes. When you have completely scanned your energy space, let the rose float up and away and burst into thousands of tiny pieces. Let all of the energy return to its source.

Now imagine a beautiful green light that surrounds and filters through your space. This light brings you balance, peace, and harmony. Finally, surround the energy space and fill it with the white rose of strength, protection, and peace. Now you are ready to proceed.

OPENING THE ENERGY DOORS

Understanding the importance of the seven main energy centers, or chakras, is essential to developing one's psychic abilities. Chakras are constantly spinning like an energy vortex, and when they are weakened through misuse or overuse, they will slow down or stop. The following exercise, if practiced on a weekly basis, will keep these centers clear and in alignment. Learning to attune to the colors of the chakras will help you to observe the colors of the aura.

Sit up straight with your feet on the floor. After thoroughly practicing your *preliminary groundwork,* close your eyes and focus your awareness on the very bottom of your spine. This is the base of the energy system known as the kundalini. As you focus here, envision a door. Imagine the door opening and the color red coming through the doorway. Imagine this center glowing like a furnace brightly burning through the doorway. The longer you watch, the more vibrant the red glow. This is your security center, where you feel safe and secure.

Now visualize the spot two inches below the navel and see another door open. This time a bright orange light radiates through the doorway. This area represents sexuality. This color dissolves any repressed emotions and guilty feelings that may be stored here.

As you move up the body, focus on the stomach and the solar plexus center. Open a door here and envision a flow of yellow color streaming forth. This is the seat of power and instinct. Feel your own power within as the color completely fills this energy center.

Now go up to the heart area and visualize another door opening with green shining through; the color green in this area heals any hurts or sadness. As the color glows brightly, feel love pulsating in every part of your body.

Move to the throat area and see another door opening, releasing a bright blue light. This chakra is the center of self-expression. This vibrant color will remind you of a clear blue sky and will free up your creativity.

Move to the area between your eyes. See another door open through which the color indigo pours. As this color intensifies, it energizes your all-knowing intuitive center.

Finally, move to the top of your head. When this door opens, a violet ray shoots out. This is your spiritual connection to the universe. You feel illuminated.

As you scan your chakra centers, see all the colors spinning in unison and blending with each other. Now envision a golden light completely surrounding and protecting you. You should feel energized, balanced, and enlightened. Take your time enjoying this exercise.

DEVELOPING INTUITION AND PSYCHIC AWARENESS

The more you practice the *preliminary groundwork,* the more fluid it should become. When you are completely comfortable with it, you will be ready for the following two meditations. Once again, get centered in your energy and place your awareness behind the center of your forehead in your third eye. Be fully conscious of your body and the energy flowing up and down the spine. The previous chakra meditation will help open you up for these practices.

The first is a simple visualization technique. Start with the *preliminary groundwork.* When you are centered and relaxed, picture yourself sitting peacefully, with a fluffy white cloud about three feet above your head. Imagine a cord pulling you out of the top of your head. Sense yourself rising out of your body, entering the cloud, and looking around from your new vantage point. As you look down from this height, you will be more aware of the world below you and the energy around you. Become aware of the feelings and impressions that you get in this cloud.

The second technique starts, again, with the *preliminary groundwork.* After you center your energy, imagine that you have a control center much like a radio inside you. As you turn on the radio, and dial to the higher numbers, your frequency increases. At this elevated rate of vibration, you are now able to detect and more thoroughly evaluate your impressions, feelings, and thoughts.

THE DEVELOPMENT CIRCLE

Purpose

The purpose of a development circle is to assist like-minded people in developing their natural psychic abilities and connections to the spiritual realm. We must acknowledge that the spirit world vibrates at a much higher frequency than our world. Therefore, the participants of a circle must increase their individual vibrations in order to integrate the thoughts, feelings, words, and sights of spirit beings. The development circle will help those involved to expand their consciousness.

Most impressions are received telepathically through mind-to-mind communication. The spirits will only send as much information as a medium can comprehend—and even then, the signal can be misinterpreted, or the information conveyed may be vague and fragmented. This is where the development part of the circle comes into play. As you sit in the circle on a regular basis, with the help of others in the circle, you learn how to discern between a thought coming from another source and one that originates in your own subconscious.

Format

There should be a minimum of four people and a maximum of twelve in a development circle. The group should consist of people who are in harmony with one another and who can work well together. To expand the group's energy, the same people should sit each week. Rarely, if ever, should a new member enter the group.

The individuals should be well balanced and share a sincere desire to serve humankind by the knowledge and awareness they receive. People who are seeking power or fame from the abilities attained in the circle should not be a part of it.

The circle should be held at the same location and in the same room every week. If possible, the development room should not be used when the group is not meeting. Members should sit in the same chairs every time the group is in session. This is to assist the spirit doctors, guides, and chemists in building the psychic energy of the group. The group should meet for a minimum of six consecutive months.

Room Preparation

Preparing the room for each session is easy, fun, and nurturing. If possible, do so at least two hours in advance. Make sure there is proper ventilation and that the temperature is comfortable. You may choose to light candles and incense—they raise the frequency of the vibrations in the room. You may also play soft music before the meeting and during the circle. The music should not be distracting. These preparations are to enhance the experience, not to detract from it.

Position the chairs so that members are facing each other in a circle. Knees do not have to touch. The chairs should be hard-backed but comfortable. There is no reason for the group to hold hands. You may have a low light on during the circle, or you may sit in complete darkness—the latter is preferable if you are attempting to experience physical manifestation.

Individual Preparation

Remember that your awareness is brought to everyone else in the circle. Therefore, during the day of your meeting, keep your thoughts loving and peaceful. Never plan anything too physically challenging on that day. If possible, make it a day of rest and reflection.

There are some very important dietary restrictions to follow on the day of a meeting. Do not eat red meat at least twenty-four hours beforehand. Meat contributes to density, and the less density a spirit has to deal with, the better. This is especially important because spirit will manipulate the solar plexus chakra of an individual, and if someone has a blocked digestive system, it may slow the process. All meals taken during the day of a development circle should be light. Don't eat for at least two hours prior to sitting in the circle.

Refrain from drinking alcohol for at least twenty-four hours before the circle. However, water is vital—

not only to hydrate the system, but for cleansing any psychic debris that might be in the system. Drink plenty of it.

Try to wear clothes made of natural fibers such as cotton. Never wear clothing that is tight or uncomfortable. Loose clothing helps facilitate the spirit doctors' and chemists' energetic work. Also, you do not want to be distracted by anything in and around your physical body.

Conducting the Circle

A circle needs a group leader. Choose someone with experience conducting circles and mediumship development. Such an individual will know how to access the energy of the members of the circle and where to position them depending on their energy. It is imperative that the leader has a vast knowledge of the energy systems of the body so that he or she can teach this to others. The leader will also train the members how to use their minds.

I believe it is important for the leader to set the energy of the room and the circle by bringing everyone together with an opening prayer. The leader might say something like the following.

> Dear spirit friends, we ask your blessing on our circle. We ask for your protection, as we blend both worlds together and sit in service of spirit. We ask you to surround this circle in the energy of eternal light and love.

Physically Speaking

I have often been asked, "Why is development such a long and tedious process?" Remember, you are not only developing your mental awareness. The endocrine and glandular systems are also being stimulated and charged. Therefore, the process must be slow and consistent. Nothing should be done so quickly as to cause harm or shock the body's systems. As the spirit doctors work on each member of the circle, any weakness in that person's body will be strengthened in order to aid in spirit contact.

I have noticed that during the first few months of several of my circles, many people seem much more emotional than normal. This is because their emotional body is being repaired, blended, and balanced with their mental, physical, and spiritual bodies. You can say it is like fine-tuning a car to get the highest possible output. Therefore, the process should be slow and deliberate. *Patience is the key.*

Inside the Circle

After the leader says an opening prayer, members should take turns saying their own prayers aloud. This will share their energy with everyone else. At the same time, each member's voice assists in raising the vibrations of the group as a whole.

Once the prayers are completed, the group should sit in silence. I recommend doing the breathing exercise to raise your thoughts to a higher level. During the breathing exercise I recommend that each person concentrate on the word *love*.

At first, you may feel the temperature change and experience a sense of moving in and out of your body. This is normal. More than likely, spirit is manipulating your auric field and energy systems. After a brief period, random thoughts may cross your mind. They may seem mindless. Do not judge them. Just experience them—let them come and go.

You may experience a variety of thoughts during development. At first, they may be normal, everyday thoughts. Soon you may notice that you are receiving impressions and thoughts that do not seem to originate in your own mind but belong to someone else. When this occurs, try to retain the messages that are transmitted from elsewhere so that at the end of the circle you can share them with fellow members.

The circle leader will feel the energy build and will know when the work is completed at each session. The leader will carefully and softly guide the members back to an awareness of the room and their bodies. Now is the time for you to share any impressions you might have experienced.

When all have finished speaking, the leader will end with a closing prayer to thank spirit for the work accomplished in that segment. Members may also say a closing prayer if they choose. As you leave the circle, you take the insights and knowledge gained through the circle to use in everyday life.

READING THE AURA

Always begin with the grounding exercise. For this exercise, the light in the room should be dim. You can work with a partner, and use a white or light-colored background behind him. Sit several feet in front of your partner and have him concentrate on sending energy out the top of his head.

If you are the person reading the aura, close your eyes. Slowly begin to open your eyes and keep them slightly out of focus. Concentrate at looking just above your partner's head until you begin to see the aura's outline. Ask your partner to send energy to other parts of his body, and observe that particular area. Notice if the energy, which may appear as a white mist, becomes more concentrated in certain areas.

To begin seeing your own aura, sit in front of a big mirror in a very low-lit room with the light behind you. Close your eyes, then open them slightly. Begin to look at the top of your head and around your shoulder area. Squint out of focus until you see a thin white vapor surround you.

Practice this exercise until you see a more definitive outline of the aura. As you continue, you will begin to see distinct energy patterns around the body.

STRENGTHENING THE AURA

The healthier we are physically, mentally, emotionally, and spiritually, the stronger the energy field that surrounds and supports us. A weakened aura is the result of poor diet, little or no exercise, not enough rest, negative emotions, stress and worry, excessive drugs and alcohol, negative thoughts, and inadequate psychic protection.

Our thoughts have an incredible effect on the aura, and like a paintbrush, a thought can be a delicate stroke or a blurry mess. The following technique, if done on a regular basis, can aid in strengthening your auric field.

After your *preliminary groundwork* exercise, imagine yourself standing in a colorful garden. Above your head is a golden sun. One of its rays touches the crown of your head and enters your body. As it moves through your body from head to toe, feel its energy and say to yourself, *I am the light of God*.

Next imagine that your body is made of see-through mesh, and that all the light streams through your body as if filtering through the holes of this mesh. Watch as the light grows brighter and stronger as it moves to each energy center, reawakening each one with its brilliance.

As the light streams out the bottom of your feet, see it swirl back up and around your body. This swirling light turns into the colors of the rainbow. It engulfs the entire body and the space beyond it. As it leaves the top of your head, repeat the affirmation, *I am the light of God*. Know that you are strengthened in that light.

PROTECTION FROM NEGATIVE THOUGHTS AND EMOTIONS

This exercise is to protect you from psychic vampires and any circumstances that deplete your energy. How do you know when to use this practice? If you feel more exhausted than usual, you may have had an encounter with a person who drained your energy. Whenever I feel a drag on my auric field, I go into what I refer to as survival mode and immediately do the following exercise.

First, I immediately get back to my center by doing the *preliminary groundwork* exercise. Then, I imagine a cone of light dropping down on each side of me, then expanding and bathing me entirely. I concentrate on being completely sealed off so that nothing of a lower energy can penetrate my force field. Then I concentrate on this light and imagine it pushing away or deflecting negative thoughts and energy. I imagine this shield sending bad vibrations back to their source. If I know exactly who is stealing my energy, and if this person is in my presence, there is an immediate, perceptible change in his or her demeanor after I conduct this exercise. She or he may start to feel uncomfortable. Most of the time the person will leave my immediate space or exit the room altogether.

CLEANSING THE AURA

There are two exceptional exercises that I perform to cleanse the aura.

The first ritual is done in the shower each morning. I stand under the jet of water and imagine that the water is a beam of golden, healing, and loving light. It comes down through and around my body and disperses any psychic debris or heavy energy from inside my body and throughout my energy field. Any energy that is not in harmony with me is washed out of the body through the toes and fingers and flows straight down the drain.

The second effective method is to envision a high-beam flashlight/vacuum cleaner. After centering, I imagine this flashlight beam in front of my head. It scans the head and shoulders. As the beam searches the area, it acts as a vacuum cleaner and sucks any unfamiliar energy into a receptacle in the back of the flashlight.

Once the receptacle is full, I imagine unscrewing the back of the flashlight and watching the debris stored there stream out and return to its source. This exercise will leave your aura shining clean. The more often this exercise is repeated, the better.

PREPARING THE AURA
FOR SPIRIT CONTACT

Most psychic activity depends very strongly on the sensitivity of the aura. Think of the aura as our own satellite dish tuning into energy waves that come into contact with it. It makes sense, therefore, that the more sensitive we are, the more we can be impressed by spirit. Sensitivity comes from discipline in the techniques I have already described. I have found that when we acquire the mind-set of a generous and open heart, it is easier to tune into the frequencies of the heaven worlds.

To help the aura open to spirit contact, begin by centering yourself with the grounding exercise. Next, use the breath as a "light meter." With every breath you inhale through your crown center, envision a golden light entering; at the same time, imagine a light meter suspended in front of you. The numbers on the meter range from one to ten. Ten is the highest frequency, or the most receptive to spirit. One is the lowest.

With each golden breath you inhale, see the light meter climb one number at a time. See the breath come in contact with each muscle, organ, and cell. When you get to the number ten, you are open and ready for spirit to send impressions.

You may substitute a stairway instead of a light meter. With every step you ascend, you become more sensitized. When you reach the tenth step at the top of the stairs, you see a door. Behind the door are spirits waiting to meet you. Open the door and greet them. Notice their physical appearance. Do you recognize them? Listen for a message from one or more of the spirits. This exercise works beautifully in tandem with opening the energy doors of the chakras.

MAKING CONTACT
THROUGH DREAMS

Very often, spirits communicate a message to us through our dreams, sending important information about ourselves and the world in which we live. How many times have you had a dream premonition that came true? Have you had the impression of having dreamed about something that you're experiencing? Do you have the same dream over and over again? Recurring dreams are definitely trying to get a message through to you. There are two exercises that I find helpful in encouraging intuition and communication in dreams.

Keep a dream journal or tape recorder next to your bed in which to record your dreams. Before you fall asleep, go through the *preliminary groundwork* exercise. Then concentrate on a question that you would like the spirit world to answer, or pose a problem that needs a solution. It could be something like: Show me where I am going with my career. Or, I ask that my spirit teacher or spirit relative reveal him/herself to me through my dreams.

Be as specific as possible and repeat your question or statements over and over until you fall asleep. The results might not occur that evening. Allow a few weeks or more for results, especially if you are a novice at dream recall. Write everything down in your dream journal the next morning, even if it is merely a feeling or a word. As you spend more and more time working with your dreams, you will find that they can be of great assistance in offering solutions to your everyday problems.

Another exercise works to achieve the same goal. First, go through the *preliminary groundwork* exercise. Next, visualize a beautiful temple on the top of the highest mountain range. Create it exactly as you would like it to appear. Design the outside and the inside as it best reflects your personality. This is your dream temple, the meeting place where the spirit world and the earth world connect. It is where reunions are made and dreams come true. Before you fall asleep, envision your dream temple and concentrate on someone you want to see, or a problem or situation that is puzzling to you. During sleep, you will reside in the temple. Once again, make sure to keep your dream journal or recorder next to your bed so that when you wake up, you can take notes on what occurred there.

AUTOMATIC WRITING

Often, one can be impressed through writing without knowing it. That is how great writers, musicians, and artists are inspired by the spirit world. You can be too.

Sit in a darkened room at a table. Have a pad and several pencils on the table. Perform your *preliminary groundwork*. If you are working with a partner, have your partner sit across from you or in another part of the room. Your partner will write something down on a piece of paper or think of something to send you telepathically.

Sit with your eyes closed or slightly opened. You may use a blindfold if you wish. While holding the pencil lightly between your fingers, visualize that you are sitting in front of a beautiful, serene lake. Everything around you is peaceful and free. Once you establish yourself at this lake, listen to whatever words come into your head and write them down.

If you are alone, you may start moving the pencil without even being conscious of doing it. When you feel as though the energy you are receiving is no longer strong and impressionable, it is time to stop.

Turn the light on and compare what you wrote with the message your partner sent.

In the beginning of the process, the letters and scribble will be illegible. Just keep practicing. Remember that spirits must get used to using you as their instrument. You are as new to them as they are to you.

DEFINING AND CLEARING SPACE IN THE HOME OR OFFICE

Usually, the first thing we do when moving into a new space—whether it be a house, office, or apartment—is to clean the space. The walls are painted, the kitchen and toilets are cleaned, and the rugs are shampooed. Perhaps we put contact paper or shelf liner in the cabinets and drawers. Why do we go through all this trouble? It's simple. We don't want to move into a new place on top of someone else's dirt. We want to create our own environment, one that is pleasing to us.

If we put this much effort on a physical level, why

don't we do it on an energy level as well? It is very important that when you live or work in an environment, you make it your own. If you do, the energy of the place will be in harmony with you. I want to share with you a technique that I have used whenever I move into a new residence. You can use this exercise even if you have lived in your home for years, as well as your office or any space that you want to keep clear of unwanted energies.

1. Begin by playing beautiful, soft music. I have used everything from gospel, classical, and choral to New Age music. Choose music that resonates with you, but nothing jarring, wild, or with negative lyrics. I would not recommend heavy metal or violent rap music. You want to clear the energy of disorder and disturbance.

2. Find the center of the space. It could be a living room or the center of an office. Consider this to be the heart of the space. This is where you will begin. You are now ready to set the energy of the space and make it your own.

3. Begin with your *preliminary groundwork*. Continue by tuning into your own auric energy field. Next, with your mind's eye, imagine your aura expanding so that it encompasses the entire space. Watch the light of your energy filling each room and energizing it. This establishes your own energy within the place. Now it is time to envision the sun shining over the building. You can even imagine the building inside the center of the sun. The energy of the sun represents the light of God—the light of pure love, joy, happiness, and peace. Next, imag-

ine the bottom of the building connected to huge tubes that anchor it to the center of the earth. See any negative, unbalanced, foreign, excess, and unwanted energies flowing through these tubes and outside as the golden sunlight continues to fill the building. Make sure that every corner is cleansed and purified and all darkness or murkiness is eliminated down those tubes.

4. The next part of this exercise is more physical. Whenever I clear a house of unwanted spirits, I use frankincense incense, a sage stick and a large white candle. Light the incense and the candle. Use an incense burner or a receptacle filled with sand to hold the incense. Place the lit candle in a holder that collects the wax and position it inside the front door, along with the incense. Next, light the sage. It will start to smoke. Let the smoke act as a neutralizing force as you enter each room with the intention of eliminating any leftover negativity. As I enter each room, I imagine sending my light into the room to remove any other person's energy from it. Go through the room and declare it your space. I usually say, "Only protection, love, and peace may enter these windows and doors." Next, walk through the room and sweep the energy toward the main door of the house where the candle is situated. Always mentally sweep the energy toward the front door. You can use the sage smoke and make sweeping gestures with your hand as if clearing the space. Go through each room completely. When you are satisfied that you have covered the entire area of your home or office, go to the candle at the front door. The candle has accumulated the negative and unwanted energies. Blow out the candle and re-

move it from the house. Throw the entire candle, wax and all, into the garbage. In this way, you are disposing of all the leftover, stagnant energy. Your space is now clean.

Remember to do all these exercises with rightmindedness. Contacting the invisible forces is not something to be done lightly or as a game to entertain your friends. You are contacting very real energies and beings on different planes of existence, and you do not want to conjure anything negative or harmful. Please do not be careless in your undertakings. Always surround yourself with the light of God before working with the invisible realms. Make sure you think positive thoughts and remain emotionally calm and poised.

If you encounter a negative astral entity in your development, always imagine the light surrounding you as a protective shield. Ask the being, "Are you from the Light?" If it is not, it will leave your space. Never do exercises after extreme physical exertion, alcohol or drug use, or anything that has drained your energy. Be aware and alert in your endeavors.

chapter 10

YOUR QUESTIONS
ANSWERED

*From Premonitions and Past Lives
to Pets and Soul Mates*

Everyone chooses a different path in life. That's what makes us unique. When embarking on a spiritual path and opening your mind and senses to the invisible world of spirit, you will be changed—of that I have no doubt. Ultimately you will be rewarded, but your rewards may not be tangible. Material gain is not the reason for existence. Many people find this hard to accept at this particular time in our society. Nevertheless, there are ordinary people who are transforming the world without even knowing it. By their kindness, positive thoughts, uplifting energy, and love, they are literally changing the consciousness of the world. It is my desire that you also decide to become a transformer and to develop your mind and psychic awareness for the enrichment of the human race.

The following questions have been asked during demonstrations, lectures, and television and radio interviews. I offer some answers here as a way of broadening and summarizing the information presented in this book.

Q: *What is an altered state of consciousness?*
A: This is a state of mind that is different from your waking consciousness—you can experience it awake or asleep. An example of an awake altered state is when you are partially withdrawn from your immediate environment while relaxing, meditating, or daydreaming. You can be totally absorbed in a book or a project and be in an altered state of consciousness.

Q: *What is the best altered state for psychic phenomena?*
A: The period just before falling asleep or waking up is often the best time to receive intuitive information. Dreams are especially important because when we sleep at night, we leave our physical bodies and meet our spirit guides to receive helpful information.

Q: *Do you have to be smart to be psychic?*
A: One does not have to have a high IQ to become proficient in psychic awareness. Sometimes people with a high intelligence can inhibit their ability at psychic phenomena because they analyze or rationalize too much.

Q: *What is the difference between a psychic, a medium, and a channel?*
A: Everyone is psychic. It is up to each one of us to develop our psychic awareness and intuition. A medium is a psychic who has fine-tuned his or her extrasensory

perception and can interface with the spirits in other dimensions. There are several types of mediums. I am a mental medium and can communicate with spirits while fully conscious. A trance medium is someone who goes into a trance state to relay messages from the other side. Channels are similar to trance mediums in that they usually go into a trance to bring forth information—they are not in an awake state and, like mediums, contact other levels of reality. The channels that are popular in this day and age usually bring through messages from beings that may or may not have lived on earth. Often the bodies of channels are taken over by these beings and speak with their voices, very similar to the way Dr. Aldrich came through me (see Chapter Two).

Q: *What is channeled material, and where does it come from?*

A: It is information that is inspired by spirit and conveyed through a medium or channel. The Seth books authored by Jane Roberts are probably the most widely read channeled material of the past thirty years. *A Course in Miracles* is another example of channeled material that is widely accepted as the words of Jesus.

Q: *Where do trance mediums go when they are in trance?*

A: Some mediums have no recall of where they are when in trance. They seem to be unconscious. Others may wander the astral world as they wait to return to their bodies.

Q: *Can I become a medium?*

A: Certain individuals are more prone to mediumship than others. Usually they must develop mediumship skills over a period of time. But it is not something that can be forced. Mediumship involves the ability to manipulate energy—mediums must be able to alter their energy levels to such an extent as to communicate with the higher vibrations of the spirit world. Psychics are not necessarily mediums, but all mediums are psychics.

Q: *What is the difference between telepathy and clairvoyance?*

A: I like to equate telepathy with sending a telegram. However, in telepathy, the message is sent from mind to mind, not over wires. A telepathist sends a message to another person, usually at a distance. A clairvoyant sees an image of an event, person, or situation that is happening in the present or has already taken place.

Q: *What is a premonition?*

A: A premonition or precognition is the intuitive sensing of a future event. This may happen as a vision, hearing the information via spirit, or through bodily sensations.

Q: *Are premonitions generally bad?*

A: Premonitions usually forewarn of impending crisis or disaster. There have been instances when a someone has canceled an airplane flight after having a premonition, and the plane *did* malfunction. Abraham

Lincoln had a premonition after he was elected the first time. He saw two images of his face in the mirror; one was normal and the other was pale and deathlike. A person who has premonitions can be of great service to others. However, be wary of someone who is a persistent harbinger of bad news.

Q: *Do premonitions generally come true?*
A: I believe a premonition is another way in which spirit warns us so that we can make different choices. However, if we become overly fearful and believe in every disastrous imagining, we can make a situation come true by our own energetic force.

Q: *Why do certain religions denounce mediums and psychics?*
A: All cultures have had their seers, soothsayers, and prophets. In ancient times these psychics took the place of modern psychologists. The condemnation of spirit communication can be traced to Moses. He declared that it was against the religious law of the time for a person to commune with spirits for reasons other than helping the nation of Israel. His pronouncement became part of Judaic law and ultimately Judeo-Christian doctrine. Moses did, however, sanction dreams and prophetic visions. The chief duty of the prophets of biblical times was to convey messages that would lead Israel out of bondage. However, I do not believe the Bible is a literal text. To me, "bondage" does not pertain to physical enslavement but rather to spiritual deficiency.

Q: *Are women better psychics than men?*

A: Women seem to be more interested in psychic awareness than men, perhaps because they are more open to their feelings and intuition. Sometimes men are better at sending information and women at receiving it. Men have the same ability to develop their psychic power as women.

Q: *What can interfere with psychic awareness?*

A: Physical illnesses, fatigue, stress, nervousness, anxiety, or intellectualizing about an outcome are all ways you can interfere with your psychic abilities.

Q: *Are creative people more psychic than others?*

A: All people are creative. However, artists, composers, writers, and actors may be more psychically aware because their work often requires an altered state of consciousness. Everyone can tap into the invisible worlds via intuition and inspirational thought. We are limited only by our own thinking.

Q: *Are children better psychics than adults?*

A: Children probably are better natural psychics, although they may have no idea what psychism is. Our society often shuts children down by telling them, "It was only a dream." Or, "It's just your imagination." Most of us are unable to help our children because our own psychic awareness is closed off. As children grow older, their memories of the heaven worlds fade away.

Q: *Can music enhance psychic experiences?*

A: I often use music in my demonstrations to help people relax and let go of their everyday concerns. When people are able to bypass their rational mind-set, it is easier to go into an altered state of consciousness. Music also stimulates the emotional body, which helps people get in touch with their feelings. Therefore, certain music is very conducive to psychic awareness.

Q: *What is spiritualism, and how did it come about?*

A: Spiritualism is communication with spirits, angels, and deceased loved ones. This form of psychic phenomena has been a part of humanity since recorded civilization. Pythagoras, one of the greatest Greek philosophers and mystics, taught that it was possible to commune with the dead. In this country, modern spiritualism was first documented in the mid-nineteenth century when two sisters, Katie and Margaret Fox, reported hearing tapping sounds in their home. They alleged that these sounds were the rappings of a person who had become an earthbound entity after being murdered in that home. In 1857 three Harvard professors were chosen to study the phenomenon of the Fox sisters. Many years later one of the sisters declared that it was all a hoax. Since that time, many charlatans have surfaced on the metaphysical scene, giving spiritualism and mediumship a bad name. By the 1920s spiritualism had reached its peak, gaining followers like the physician and writer Sir Arthur Conan Doyle and the international couture designer Elsa Schiaparelli. In the mid-1960s spiritualism again received notoriety when

Bishop James Pike of the Episcopal Church communicated with his son who had committed suicide. He wrote his account in the book *The Other Side*.

Q: *Do mediums work only in the dark?*
A: The majority do not. Physical mediumship is the only mediumship that requires the dark. Because I am a mental medium, my demonstrations are done with the lights on as bright as possible. The energy of the light helps me to sustain the energy of spirit in the room. When you are first learning to contact spirits, as in a development circle, it may help to keep the lights dim so that the outside environment will not be distracting. However, darkness is not necessary for spirit activity.

Q: *Can mediums decipher messages from someone who speaks a foreign language?*
A: Language is a limitation of the physical world. Spirit communication is through thought. Thoughts are not restricted to a particular language.

Q: *How can I tell if a psychic is fake or real?*
A: You must use discernment in all undertakings. Hopping from one psychic to another hoping to get answers for life's problems is not going to work. You must learn to cultivate your mind and intuition, read and study a variety of spiritual philosophies, and perhaps even attend classes to learn to rely on your own intuitive ability.

Q: *How do you shut off spirits when you don't want to hear them?*

A: I have to shut down my energy systems. When I communicate with the spirit world, I open my chakra systems and raise my energy level to meet spirit's higher frequency. When I am finished with the communication, I close the doors of my chakras so that I am free to do other things and spirits will not disturb me.

Q: *Do you foretell the future?*

A: One must realize that there is no such thing as time in the world of spirit. Time relates only to the physical world as a measure of progress. Spirits measure things as events. I may tell of an event that has already occurred or that will occur in the future.

Q: *Do you tell embarrassing things to someone when you do a reading?*

A: I am not responsible for the information; I relay it. I am the telephone, if you will. If a spirit feels the information is important, then I will communicate it and sometimes it can be embarrassing. I try my best to be discreet and discerning and do not relate information that is harmful to another.

Q: *How can we become more discerning?*

A: First, you must develop discipline of mind by paying attention to your thoughts. By weeding out negativity, judgments, and other people's opinions, you free yourself from limited thinking. The next step is to be honest about your feelings. Know why you feel a certain way about something. Then you can distinguish what you are feeling from what others are feeling. Over time, you will develop discernment through trial and error and effort. As you learn to seek balance in all that you do, you will have a better understanding of the world around you. As you listen to your own inner voice, you will not only know better, but you can also do better.

Q: *What is a poltergeist?*
A: A poltergeist is a psychic disturbance, such as an object flying around a room, or a door slamming shut. Poltergeists can be attributed to earthbound spirits that are trying to get the attention of the living. Sometimes the phenomenon is caused by the energy of someone in the house who is disturbed or overstimulated. Teenagers, especially, can cause poltergeist phenomena due to sudden changes in their hormonal levels.

Q: *Why do ghosts haunt houses?*
A: Spirits usually return to their old surroundings—especially if they left earth suddenly or violently or with unfinished business. Murder victims, accident victims, and anyone who died in a traumatic way will return to the scene of their deaths. These souls are earthbound and not fully aware of what has happened to them. People who were terribly unhappy on earth may also linger around their homes. Sometimes spirits will return to warn someone they love of an illness or danger.

Q: *What is psychometry?*
A: In psychometry, a person holds an object and is

impressed with feelings or visions about the person to whom the object belongs. Everyone and every object has energy, and the vibrations of an object can often reveal the history of its owner. Psychometry is used a lot in criminal investigation. Psychics skilled at psychometry have often been able to help police find missing persons or murderers by holding an object found at the scene of a crime.

Q: *How do drugs, alcohol, and psychedelic substances affect our psychic power?*

A: Such substances may increase your sensing ability and can indeed induce an altered state, visions, and astral travel. However, I do not recommend that people use these methods of opening themselves to spirit, for several reasons. First, these substances are uncontrollable. One may not be aware of the entities that they may attract. Also, development is a gradual process. You must be patient and open your intuitive side in the proper way over a period of time so as not to cause any physical problems or psychological concerns. If you do not have the proper guidance or control in opening and closing your energy centers (both of which you lose by using drugs to gain entry to the spirit realm), you could experience mental breakdown, schizophrenia—severe mental illness.

Q: *When I dream of someone who has passed over, is it really the person?*

A: Dreams are the most common venue for spirits to make themselves known. If the dream image looks and acts like the person when he or she was on earth and the characteristics and personality match, then ⸻ robably is that person. If not, it may be someone in the astral world masquerading as a loved one. When in doubt, always ask the person if he or she is from God or the Light.

Q: *How can I tell if my dream is of a psychic nature?*

A: All dreams are of a psychic nature. A dream that is vivid, colorful, and emotionally charged may be more psychically significant than normal. Also, if one is the observer rather than a participant, the dream may be a premonition or precognitive dream.

Q: *Did Jesus perform miracles?*

A: Miracles are extraordinary acts. Jesus was a master teacher, an Essene adept, and a highly evolved soul, proficient at manipulating molecules of energy. His ability to turn water into wine and help the blind to see could be quite possible. However, we must remember that the parables in the Bible were not meant to be literal. The miracles attributed to Jesus are actually spiritual metaphors. As Jesus said, "What I can do, you can do also."

Q: *Can we remember past lives?*

A: When I talk about past lives, people usually like to think they were some outstanding figure in history like Cleopatra or Napoleon. However, that is highly unlikely. When contemplating who you might have been in a past life, look to your present life. The skills and traits that you bring to this life are ones that you have developed in others. Your likes, tastes, and interests are recorded in your soul throughout every lifetime. As you evolve, your interests and traits also evolve. We are all here to complete a karmic debt or unfinished business from other lifetimes. We know this when we meet someone that we seem to have known before. We have flashes of déjà vu and know that we have been in a certain place before. As we develop and expand our awareness, the veil between the physical world and the limitless universe becomes transparent, and we are able to detect parts of lives that we have lived before.

Q: *Why is it difficult to remember a past life?*

A: The memory of our past lives is stored in our subconscious. It is difficult to detect these lives because this part functions at a level below conscious awareness. As we begin to open the doors to our own innate awareness through meditation and visualization, we will begin to tap into our subconscious thoughts. Eventually, with commitment and practice, we will begin to recognize that the traits and characteristics that define us in this life have been a part of our lives in the past.

Q: *How do you know if a past life is not merely a figment of your imagination?*

A: If you think you were some heroic figure of the past, it is probably wishful thinking. Most past lives are ordinary, sometimes even dull. Your present life often offers clues to your past. An affinity for a particular country or language may suggest that you have lived there before. An exceptional ability to play a musical instrument or a sport at an early age may also be evidence of bringing talents from other lives into the current one. Fears and phobias that have no basis in this lifetime may be carryovers from a past lifetime. The best way to discern your past lives is to know yourself in this one.

Q: *Were my relatives a part of my past life?*

A: Many times, family members are linked together by karmic bonds based on previous incarnations. Before coming to earth, we decide to share our experiences with others with whom we have journeyed through life once before. By understanding and sharing in both joys and sorrows, we learn more about one another and ourselves.

Q: *Do spirits retain a memory of their lives on earth?*

A: People who pass from this earthly stage seem to retain their most recent physical life experience, along with the same personality and sensibilities that they possessed in the physical form. After a spirit sheds its etheric body at death, it resides in an astral form. In this spirit form, a spirit will realize that it is a spiritual being composed of the sum of all of its lifetime experiences. It remembers the recent lifetime as one of many. Also be aware that earth is not the only place where one can experience life, and that life is not always expressed in human form.

Q: *What is psychic healing?*

A: Psychic healing is a form of healing that uses universal energy to bring about balance, harmony, and curative measures. Forms of this type of healing include prayer, the laying on of hands, meditation, shamanism, mental treatment, and psychic surgery. The person receiving the healing may experience the sensation of heat in the area of the body where the healing is taking place. Sometimes a healer can temporarily feel the person's pain and absorb the symptoms as the diseased energy leaves the body.

Q: *In automatic writing, where do the messages come from?*

A: Usually the communication comes from a discarnate spirit or the unconscious mind of the writer. The messages can also be telepathic—sent from one living being to another. Usually a spirit guide will relay messages through automatic writing. I often think that many of our great works of music and literature were created through automatic writing.

Q: *Is psychic power a lifetime gift?*

A: Psychic power is a natural part of who you are. If recognized and utilized, this awareness can empower you and expand your experiences. It is available whenever you want it. It is up to you to use it or let it remain dormant.

Q: *What do you mean when you talk about the law of affinity, or "like attracts like"?*

A: We actually create our environment with our thoughts and with what we imagine will happen. This is what I mean by like attracts like. This law of affinity is set, and there is no getting around it. Remember that you have control over your thoughts. If you want to attract peaceful, loving, comfortable, and cheerful experiences, you have to give out what you want to get. You cannot be rude, judgmental, critical, unfeeling, and careless and expect to receive kindness in return. You must give out the qualities you want to receive. That is the way it goes.

Q: *Do animals have psychic awareness?*

A: Animals have instinct, which is akin to our psychic awareness. The emotional closeness of animals to humans seems to stir up psychic communication between the two. Domesticated animals can often sense when a person is sick, dying, or in trouble. Animals are the greatest teachers of unconditional love and are often angels in disguise.

Q: *Do animals have souls and survive death like humans?*

A: Yes, of course they do. They, too, are souls made of energy. Energy does not die; it only changes form. Our pets and other animals pass into the spiritual realms and are usually surrounded by family members or tended by animal keepers who share an affinity with them.

Q: *Can an animal be cured through psychic healing?*

A: Yes, in the same way a human can be healed. Animals have been cured through the laying on of hands as well as by prayer. Remember that everything is energy, and the bond between a pet and its owner is much like that of parent and child. Therefore, your thoughts of love are especially powerful and have a positive healing effect on your pets.

Q: *How does a pet know if its master is going to die?*

A: Pets have an abundance of psychic awareness. Their awareness is not censored by criticism and opinion. When a pet's owner is about to die, the pet will often behave differently. It may not eat for days. If a person is sick and in bed, the pet may curl up on the bed to give that person comfort. I have known pets to react from a distance. For instance, if its owner dies in a hospital, a dog may bark or howl wildly, knowing that its owner is gone.

Q: *What is an out-of-body experience?*

A: When we go to sleep at night, we die to the physical world. We leave our bodies from the top of our heads and stay connected to them through a silver cord that is attached to our solar plexus area. This cord is unbreakable and allows us to travel the astral worlds while our bodies remain in bed. This is an out-of-body experience. The habit of saying bedtime prayers came about because of the need to protect oneself when leaving the body at night. The astral world is full of beauty and disguise. Our spirit guides and angels are always with us to protect us. Sometimes we can leave our bodies at will when not asleep. As we leave the body, we may feel like we are traveling through a tunnel or swirling and tumbling through space. We experience enormous freedom out of the physical body and a heightened consciousness—a connection to all beings everywhere. When we die, the astral body rises out of the physical body and the silver cord is severed.

Q: *Do people leave their bodies when they are in surgery?*

A: Yes, this is quite common. Often after anesthesia has been administered, a person will rise out of his body and look down at it from the ceiling, sometimes seeing a silver cord, which appears like a ribbon extending from the body. Patients can hear the conversations of the doctors and nurses in the operating room. Nowadays doctors play music in surgery, which is quite beneficial to the patient. Sometimes patients are reluctant to return to their bodies because they are free of pain in their astral bodies. Many people return with knowledge of what it is like to die and are never afraid of death again. Dr. Raymond Moody has written of these out-of-body experiences in many books, notably *Life After Life* and *The Light Beyond*.

Q: *Is it safe to go out of the body?*

A: It is not recommended for psychic amateurs or for unstable or emotionally disturbed people. I do not recommend that people undertake astral travel unless they are fully aware of all the possibilities that await them in the astral world.

Q: *Do plants have emotions?*

A: There is a wonderful book entitled *The Secret Life of Plants* that describes how plants feel. Also the people of a community in Findhorn, Scotland, have re-

ported that they were able to establish a rapport
between themselves and the plant kingdom. We must
remember that plants are living beings and are conscious—perhaps not in the same way that humans are.
But they can cry and feel pain, just like us. I recommend
that you talk to your plants and give them the same love
and attention you would your pets. They will reward
you many times over.

Q: *I want to meet that special someone. Can I do it
through my psychic ability?*
A: I often tell people to write down the qualities of
the person with whom they want to have a love relationship. Writing helps to focus the mind, and at the
same time helps you to be specific in your request. Remember that a relationship is a learning experience. Ask
yourself, "What do I want to learn about myself in this
situation?" Always include a request that the relationship
be for your highest good. Do not obsess over the results.
Just let go and let God do the rest. Make sure that this is
what you really want, as you will be dealing with the
consequences of what you have created through your
desire.

Q: *How can I determine if a person is my soul mate?*
A: You do not have one soul mate. You have many
soul mates in your lifetime who are a part of your soul
group. More than likely, many of your soul mates are in
your life right now or will be in the future. Soul mates
can be friends, relatives, husbands, wives, co-workers,
and lovers. They appear in our lives to teach and guide us

through a variety of different circumstances. Even a troubled relationship can be two soul mates working out a karmic obligation.

Q: *If I have a difficult boss or co-worker, how can I deal with him on a psychic level?*

A: You need to center yourself and go within through meditation. Once in this quiet space, become aware of your higher God-self. Next, visualize the person with whom you are having difficulty and communicate with him through this higher self. Discuss the situation and the feelings that you are experiencing. Listen for the person's reply. Doing this will help you to have a more enlightened understanding of the other person as well as of yourself. Another method is to visualize your coworker with the light of love embracing his auric field. This creates a more loving space around the person and helps him to appreciate his own divinity. If you do this on a daily basis, you will begin to see the situation between the two of you change.

Q: *Is it psychically possible to know if someone is telling the truth?*

A: Yes. Once you develop and trust your own inner guidance, you can easily distinguish the false signals from the genuine.

Q: *Can we escape our past karma?*

A: Life is complex. Whether you believe that you have lived before or not, you are a conscious being. It is your consciousness, or unconsciousness, that creates your life experiences. I believe that as spiritual beings, we are always growing and evolving in awareness, and we reincarnate to accumulate knowledge. Earth is our classroom, and we are the pupils. We decide what we want to learn and are given opportunities to do so. Sometimes we wonder why bad things happen to good people. I do not believe that the great universal power would select people at random to bestow upon them all the good things of life while leaving others to flounder and fail. I believe that we are here to create a balance with past experiences in which we harmed others or ourselves. The motive behind today's good deeds should not be to erase past karma but rather to create a life of goodness and enlightenment while not accumulating more karma to equalize later. I also believe that we don't have to wait until another life to be rewarded for the goodness we create in this one.

Q: *Do you recommend fasting to improve psychic awareness?*

A: Fasting can help you achieve an altered state of consciousness, but it is not necessary. I recommend that you eat in moderation, but you do not have to suffer to attain enlightenment. Before attempting any psychic development, I recommend that you eat lightly and abstain from foods that are dense and of low vibration, like red meat. After your psychic development experiments you may have a glass of wine, but I do not recommend one before. Drink plenty of water at all times.

Q: *What is cosmic consciousness?*

A: This term means "conscious of the universe or cosmos." Each one of us is made up of several selves. Our higher self is completely aware and in sync with the universal consciousness. The more we attune ourselves to this higher self, the more we awake to an understanding of the universality of life and the connection between everyone and everything.

Q: *How can I overcome an obsession?*

A: Obsession is a psychological fixation on an idea, a person, or a thing. Obsessing over something actually impedes the natural flow of energy. When we are literally "fixing" an idea, it has no room to move or expand. If you have a goal, state clearly what it is, write it down, and then let it go. The universe will carry it through in the right time and in the right place. Have faith in yourself and trust that all your needs are met.

Q: *How can we live a spiritual life in this materialistic society?*

A: By being true to ourselves, we are emancipated from the illusions of the material world. Material possessions are wonderful to have and enjoy. They are tools that can help us to learn about ourselves and our priorities. However, they do not determine who we are. Only the spirit inside you is the truth. The more you can identify with this truth in every experience and every encounter, the more you can progress. The amount of love that you create will sustain you in this life and those to follow.

EPILOGUE

What we perceive with our five senses is only the tip of the iceberg. Imagine a perspective from an airplane, thirty thousand feet above the earth. Millions of people share this perspective every day. Our perspective of life changes at that altitude. We see a much bigger world than we do in our automobiles. You might say that the world has expanded, yet nothing has changed except our viewpoint.

The same is true about the relationships and situations we experience. The only thing that we can change is our perspective of these things. When we realize that our attitudes of ignorance, selfishness, competitiveness, and fear create negative results in our lives, we have a choice to alter our thoughts and beliefs. If we choose to free our minds of past conditioning and predisposed expectations, we will see life from a whole new point of view, one that is filled with the light and splendor of spirit. Then, instead of misery, we will create conditions and experiences of a positive nature as we develop into high-minded and loving individuals. From this new altitude we will discover our true selves deep within our hearts. I believe that when this happens, we will truly begin to live life.

Most of us have been programmed to see life as divided into separate parts—family, job, money, relationships, creativity, religion, and so on. This leads to feelings of isolation. But we are all connected, even if we are not aware that we are. Once we start to reawaken our God-given instincts and use all the tools afforded us, we will begin to find the connections that we have been searching for. We will radiate our truth in all that we do, bringing fullness to every aspect of life's experiences.

Remember that we are on a journey through life that is one of balance between the illusions of the material world and the truth that is spirit. We are all spiritual beings on a journey to enlightenment. By piercing the veil of illusion and tapping into the great God-connectedness of the universe, we will discover that the consciousness of heaven and earth is *one*.

ABOUT THE AUTHOR

James Van Praagh is arguably the most famous and successful spiritual medium of our time, world-renowned for his extraordinary ability to communicate with the spirits of men, women, children, and animals who have died. His lectures, demonstrations, and spiritual tours have drawn many thousands of people in the United States and abroad. He has been a featured guest on *The Oprah Winfrey Show, Larry King Live,* and countless other television and radio shows, as well as being interviewed in *The New York Times, People* magazine, and elsewhere. He lives in the Los Angeles area.

To learn more about the author's work and appearances, you may find information on his Web site:

www.VanPraagh.com

or write to:

Spiritual Horizons, Inc.
P.O. Box 60517
Pasadena, California 91116